WORKING W

PRECIOUS
METAL
CLAY

WORKING WITH
PRECIOUS METAL CLAY

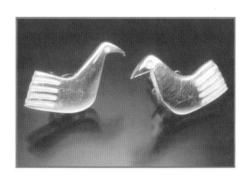

TIM MCCREIGHT

A & C Black . London

First published in Great Britain 2000
A&C Black Publishers Limited
38 Soho Square
London W1D 3HB
www.acblack.com

Reprinted 2003, 2007

ISBN 978-0-7136-5828-6

Published in the USA by
Brynmorgen Press
One Longfellow Square
Portland, Maine 04101

A CIP catalogue record for this book is available from the
British Library.

Cover designed by Dorothy Moir.

Printed and bound in Hong Kong by Elegance Printing Company Ltd.

About This Book

There is a right way and a wrong way to use this book. If what you find here helps you enjoy using PMC, that's the right way. If it slows you down or limits your creativity, please find another way to use it.

The first section (on cream-colored pages), illustrates 50 projects through step-by-step instructions. If you follow the directions, you'll make that particular piece and simultaneously learn some specific skills. Once you have a feeling for the material, you might want to alter the designs to suit your personal style. You can patch together ideas from several projects, or simply start from scratch.

In the second section (the blue pages), information is organized according to the techniques, materials and tools being discussed. In some cases, this will duplicate or overlap the methods discussed in the projects. The hope is that by presenting the information in several ways, it will be clear to a wide audience.

Table of Contents

Part One
50 Projects

Part Two
Technical Tips

Part Three
Tools You Can Make

Appendix

Acknowledgments

Most books are a collective effort and that's particularly true when the subject is a brand new material like Precious Metal Clay. Hardly a week goes by that something new doesn't come along, from a handy gadget to a radically new process. A few of these I've discovered all by myself (probably simultaneously with dozens of other people) and others have come from a generous and enthusiastic community.

It is impossible to thank each of the people who have contributed to this book, not only because the list would be long, but because in many cases ideas have come to me second-hand so I don't know to whom I owe the debt. But I would be remiss if I did not take this opportunity to thank a few specific individuals whose marks they will see throughout these pages.

In Japan, Akira Nishio, Naoki Uchiyama and Juichi Hirasawa of Mitsubishi Materials Corporation have been consistently generous with their support and resources. Among the dozens of artists I have relied on for advice, I am proud to include Celie Fago, Dana Carlson, Barbara Simon, Chris Ramsay, CeCe Wire, Chris Darway and J. Fred Woell. At Rio Grande, the American distributor of PMC, I have been helped by many people, among them Alan Bell, Kevin Whitmore, Ramona Marshall and Gary Young.

All the people at Brynmorgen Press have been a pleasure to work with, from the office staff to the editorial team. My son Jeff made the watercolor drawings, converting my thin sketches to rich illustrations. Aaron Cheever helped with the page design and undertook the complex task of making each page work as an independent visual statement. Robert Diamante has once again come to my aid with his lovely photographs, as usual making the work look its best. For office help and a resuscitating sense of humor, we all want to thank Debé Loughlin. And, at the end of the day, it is Jay I want to come home to.

Thanks, everybody!

Tim McCreight

Portland, Maine
April 2000

Introduction

There are three kinds of cooks. One type follows a recipe exactly, one type never opens a cookbook and in between are the people who use a cookbook for guidance, staying close to the recipe when they're uncertain and adding their own flourishes as they gain confidence. If that sounds like you, I think you'll like this book.

Working with Precious Metal Clay uses 50 projects to introduce the techniques and strategies of this amazing new material. In each case the sequential instructions and informative illustrations will lead you through the process from beginning to end. Along the way you'll learn how to cut, model, texture and assemble all sorts of objects, from simple earrings to complicated vessels. While you're welcome to copy these designs exactly, you might want to combine techniques from several projects to invent your own way of working. One of the great things about PMC is its incredible versatility. Each person will develop his or her own style of working — and nothing in this book should get in the way of that.

In addition to the projects, you will find 25 techniques described in Part Two. These include information that applies to all work such as construction tricks, rehydrating techniques, polishing and coloring procedures. You'll want to visit this section periodically as your skills advance. In Part Three you'll find 10 tools you can make for yourself. These can all be bought from jewelry supply companies, so don't worry if you're not the Do-It-Yourself type.

I've written other books about jewelrymaking, but they dealt with techniques that were centuries old. Precious Metal Clay was developed only a few years ago, an eye blink as these things go. Many of the ideas presented here did not exist when I started this book; and even as I send this to print I know there are exciting developments just around the corner.

Isn't that GREAT!

The PMC Toolbox

Blades
Tissue Blade
Ruler
Credit Card
Playing Card
Thin Copper, Brass or Steel
X-Acto

Modeling Tools
Paint Brushes (hard and soft bristle)
Color Shaper
Dental Tools
Craft Stick
Tongue Depressor
Plastic Straws and Stirrers
Toothpicks
Small Dowels
Rolling Pin
Clay Tools
Needle Tool

Miscellaneous
Plastic Templates
Compass/Divider
Magnifiers
Pliers - chain-nose, round-nose
Olive Oil
Water Container
Texture Samples - bark, leaves, lace, etc.
Tweezers

Firing
Shelves
Gloves
Spatula
Bricks
Vermiculite
Terra-cotta Dish

Finishing
Salon Boards
Sandpaper
Sanding Pads
Blackening Agent
Rouge Cloth
Polishing Stick

PMC Basics

Readers who have some experience with silver clay may feel comfortable skipping over this section but it is suggested reading for first-time users. Precious Metal Clay is surprisingly simple to use (even a grown-up can do it!) but there are a few basic tips that will make working with PMC more efficient and enjoyable.

It is helpful to understand the three ingredients that comprise PMC. The largest portion is a pure metal that has been cut into extremely fine particles. PMC can be made with pure platinum, pure gold and pure silver. The metal is cut so small that the result could be described as a flour. If you held a handful of silver powder it would feel like talc — that's how small the particles are.

The second ingredient (only a small percentage) is an organic binder. This is a proprietary material, but for our purposes we can think of it as something like cornstarch. It is a naturally occurring, non-toxic powder. The balance, about 10-20%, is water.

The proportion of the three components has been carefully determined after many experiments. The silver and binder are stable (won't be changed by handling) but water will of course evaporate, especially in heat or dry air. The first rule is to minimize this. Do not unwrap the PMC until you are ready to use it and then take out only what you need. Avoid working in a draft or under a hot lamp. As you work, get in the habit of periodically adding a few drops of water to refresh the clay. Be careful not to add too much — PMC can easily become slimy if it gets too wet.

Before handling PMC, put a small amount of olive oil in your palm and spread it over your hands. This will coat the PMC as you work and seal it somewhat against evaporation. The oil will also prevent the PMC from sticking to your fingers or tools.

TOOLS

A lot of the fun of PMC is that the tools are so simple. You will want a piece of plastic pipe for a rolling pin, a clay needle and various modeling tools that you can buy from ceramic dealers or make yourself. I do most of my work with odds and ends I've picked up around the house like toothpicks, nails, popsicle sticks, knitting needles, pens, etc. Add a small watercolor brush and a razor knife and you are ready to get started. Your collection will probably grow as you gain experience.

The only two materials to avoid as you set up your work space are cardboard and aluminum. The first will draw moisture out of the clay and the other will contaminate it with nasty oxide. I like to work on a piece of plastic sheet as described on page 79.

ASSEMBLY

Most projects are relatively simple to put together. You will typically roll out a sheet, perhaps texture it, cut out a desired shape and bend it into a form, sometimes attaching several units together. In many cases you simply press the parts firmly against one another to make a joint. If the clay is dry or when the point of contact is small, add a drop of water at the joint. Allow it a few seconds to penetrate, then press the pieces together and close the joint with a fingertip, a brush or pointed tool. Another technique is to paint a little slip (page 81) or extrudable PMC (page 82) onto the joint before pressing the parts together. If in doubt, leave extra material at a joint or on a seam; it's easy to sand away extra after the piece is dry. If you need to stop part way through a piece, brush or spray it with water and wrap it in plastic film.

DRYING
When assembly is complete, set the work to dry where it won't get bumped. Most pieces will dry naturally in a few hours, but the process can be hastened with a hair dryer or heat lamp. To allow air to circulate freely, I often set completed work on plastic mesh, rumpled up tissue paper, or a piece of foam rubber.

It's not uncommon for pieces to warp as they dry, especially if they are thin or have varying thickness. This is not a problem. Often the distortion will straighten out during firing and, if it doesn't, the work can be pressed flat after it has been fired.

FIRING
More information on this important topic is given on page 94, but a quick description is in order here. When work is dry, place it in an electric kiln (also called a furnace) and heat it to a point where the metal particles fuse together. PMC is available in three versions, each of which has its own firing sequence. The full spectrum runs from 2 hours at 900° C (1650° F) to as little as 600° C (1110° F) for 30 minutes — turn to page 94 for details. Longer exposure to the heat does no harm, but shortening firing time will leave the metal weak.

Silver clay can be fired in any kiln that will reliably reach and maintain the desired temperature. Kilns used for enameling, burnout, glass tempering and test firing will all work. A small, efficient furnace with a programmable thermostat is an ideal choice, both for convenience and assured success. Once the kiln is loaded and the programming set, a touch of a button will heat the furnace to temperature, sustain a constant temperature and shut off after a set time. These furnaces quickly pay for themselves through their reliable convenience.

FINISHING
After firing, only one of the three ingredients remains — pure metal, either silver or gold. PMC objects can be handled like any other silver work. In most cases the PMC is burnished or sanded, sometimes blackened to create contrast and polished with a rouge cloth. PMC can be soldered, riveted, electroplated, enameled and sandblasted. For detailed information on each of these topics, see the appropriate topic headings in Part Two.

Part One
50 Projects

Leaf with Pearl

Cut a leaf shape from a sheet of PMC about as thick as a nickel (6 playing cards, 2 mm). Use a plastic ruler or similar blunt tool to press a groove down the center for the vein. Rock back and forth slightly to make a gentle trough.

Roll out a snake of PMC about twice as long as the leaf, tapering at one end.

Dampen the groove with water and press the tapered rod into it so that some extends past the top of the leaf. Roll the part of the stem that sticks out to flatten it slightly. This will be bent around after firing to make the loop from which the pendant will hang.

Press lines into the leaf with a ruler, card or blade.

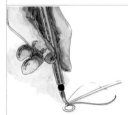

Make a round loop at the tip of the leaf, either using the vein or by adding a small PMC thread.

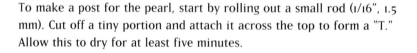

To make a post for the pearl, start by rolling out a small rod (1/16", 1.5 mm). Cut off a tiny portion and attach it across the top to form a "T." Allow this to dry for at least five minutes.

Invert the "T" unit and attach it across the round loop. The goal is to have a rod that spans the loop with a short post sticking up vertically from the center to hold the pearl. Fire and finish as recommended by the manufacturer.

After firing and polishing, bend the stem with round-nose pliers to make the pendant loop. Trial fit the pearl; snip the wire with fingernail clippers if it's too long. Use a drill bit in your fingers if the hole in the pearl needs to be made bigger. Glue the pearl onto the post with epoxy (see page 103).

Bouquet

This project takes advantage of the 28% shrinkage of PMC to make a wonderfully detailed surface. Get ready to work small and let the firing make your precise modeling even more impressive!

Roll out a ball of PMC no bigger than a pea. Press the ball onto a playing card — this makes it easy to rotate the flower as you work. Press the ball flat to make a disk about as thick as a nickel (6 cards, 2 mm). Use a sharp edge (blade, ruler, card) to segment the disk into wedges, pressing no more than halfway through.

File a popsicle stick to the shape of a blunt chisel. Press the tool into the perimeter at each line to create a scalloped edge that will define the petals of the blossom. The effect is more dramatic if the tool is angled so the notch is slightly undercut.

Press into the center of the flower with a rounded tool like the tip of a paint brush handle or a pen. This crater will force the petals outward. Refine the shape with the chisel tool as needed. Set the blossom aside and make several more in the same way, varying the size.

Roll out a thin sheet of PMC for a base. Moisten a spot on the slab and transfer one of the flowers onto the base. Press a small round tool (e.g., the tip of a paintbrush handle) into the center of the flower. This secures the flower to the base and simultaneously bends the flower into an interesting shape, especially when the blossoms are overlapped. Continue in this way, adding to the base to make an attractive arrangement. When it looks good — and this could be any number of flowers — use a knife or needle to cut around the outside.

Add details in the center of each blossom with a needle tool.

Gently turn the piece over to add a loop for a chain. Dampen a spot on the back of the pendant at the top and press a flat strip of PMC into place. At this point, the strip sticks out from the pendant like the handle of a frying pan. Smooth the joint so it blends in completely. Roll a small cylinder of paper to support the loop as it dries. Lay the paper in place and curl the strip back onto the pendant. Cut it off and smooth the joint. The paper can be removed after the piece is dry or left to burn away during firing.

Fire and finish as recommended.

Rubber Stamp Pendant

Rubber stamps are available in thousands of images and patterns and a wide range of sizes. Stamps that have been used with ink will do no harm to PMC — the ink will simply burn away during the firing. In the example shown here, a simple stamp is cut from a pencil eraser to decorate the background. A single letter is intentionally clipped and staggered to make a more interesting composition.

To make a background tool, cut the eraser of a new pencil into a square shape, slicing off the four sides with a razor knife. With the same sharp blade, cut a V-groove in the middle of the top. Rotate the pencil 90 degrees and cut another groove at a right angle to the first. These grooves do not have to be very deep.

Roll out a slab of PMC at least as thick as a nickel (6 cards, 2 mm). Make this about a third larger than the intended size of your pendant to allow for shrinkage. Cut away two edges of the slab of PMC to leave a square corner.

Set your eraser stamp about 3 mm from a corner. (Tip: lay a paper match along the edge as a guide). Press a row of marks that will create a patterned background while simultaneously making a smooth raised frame. Go across the top, down the side and across the bottom edge to mark out the square, then start filling in toward the center. Don't panic if the pattern bunches up or overlaps — that's part of the look. Cut away the two remaining sides to make a square.

Roll out another slab of PMC about as thick as the first one and press your rubber stamp into it. Here I'm using stamps from a children's set I bought at a toy store. If you don't like your first try, roll the PMC into a ball, make a new sheet and try again. Cut the second square with a knife or card.

Set the smaller panel onto the first one. Press it down lightly.

Cut out a shape and attach it to the top to make a loop, where the cord will attach. Roll out a strap of PMC about 1/4" wide and 3/4" long (6 x 19 mm). Attach one end to the back, centered along the top edge. Flip the pendant over and attach the other end so a loop is formed. It might be helpful to set a small rolled-up paper in the loop to hold it open while the PMC dries.

Fire as recommended. Finish by hand burnishing, tumbling or with abrasives as described on pages 100-102. Add a cord or chain.

Medallion with Stone

The use of beautifully colored stones in jewelry probably traces back to that moment when some early ancestor bent down to pick up a glistening pebble from a brook. Things have come a long way since then, but our fascination with stones remains the same. Some natural stones can withstand the heat of firing PMC, but most will discolor or break. To achieve consistently positive results, use "laboratory grown" gem stones. These are sophisticated modern creations that mimic the chemical composition of gems in nature. Stone dealers will clearly identify these gems, which are available in a wide range of colors.

Make a ball of PMC about the size of a large peanut (1/3", 8 mm in diameter) and flatten it by pinching to make a miniature pancake. Pull off another piece of PMC much smaller than the first, roll it into a ball, flatten it slightly then set it into the center of the first piece. Divide it into decorative segments with a blade or the edge of a card.

Roll another piece of PMC into a small ball roughly one-fourth the size of the original lump. Poke a pencil point or similar tool into the center of the lump and rotate it to make a conical hole for the faceted stone. Use a beverage straw to remove a plug of PMC from the bottom of this hole.

Drop the stone into place in the hole, then press it down deeply into the medallion. The stone must be seated well below the surface so that when the material around it shrinks, it will not squeeze the stone out.

Roll out a rod of PMC and cut off six equal segments, then roll each piece between your palms to make balls about 1/8" in diameter. Cut scallops on the edge of the disk with a drinking straw. Dampen each location with a paintbrush or paint on a dab of PMC paste and set a ball into place. Repeat around the form.

Press one ball flat and poke a hole through it with a needle. Add a decorative line around the edge with a needle or stamp.

Allow the piece to dry and fire as recommended. Insert a loop and attach a chain.

Ceramic Shard in a Bezel

This project introduces three new ideas: firing to create a specific shape, hammering a texture after firing and soldering a sterling element onto fired PMC. The example uses a broken piece of crockery but the technique applies equally to shells, glass, and other beautiful ornaments that can't withstand firing temperatures.

To hold the desired shape we'll need to first create a replica of the shard in plaster of Paris. Mix the white plaster powder with water to the consistency of gravy and pour it into a paper cup to a depth of about 1/2". Allow to dry for at least an hour, preferably overnight. Trace the shard onto the plaster and cut around it. Trim to size by scraping or filing to create a form that has the same size and shape as the shard.

Determine the pre-fired size of the setting for the shard, either by using the PMC Ruler on page 91 or by photocopying the ceramic piece at 130%. Work on this enlarged drawing to make the piece.

Roll out a sheet of PMC for the back of the pendant and another for the bezel wall. Moisten the joints, then press the wall onto the base. Add some slip on the inside to reinforce the joint. Trim away the PMC around the form, leaving about 1/8" (3 mm) as a border. To accommodate the stresses that will occur on the back, slice a pattern of cuts in the area that will be covered by the shard.

Set the plaster form into the center of the bezel and fire as usual. As the PMC shrinks, it will contract into the plaster and go no further. After firing, the plaster form can be chipped out with any convenient tool. If the piece is quenched while hot, the plaster will shatter and fall out.

Set the pendant on an anvil or similar resilient surface and strike a stamping tool with a light hammer to create a pattern of parallel lines.

Construct a bail from pieces of sterling wire and solder this to the PMC with silver solder or a low-temperature soft solder like STA-BRITE. Use the appropriate flux and solder. As the piece approaches soldering temperature, move the flame away so the work is just hot enough for the solder to flow. Because they are less porous, PMC+ and PMC3 are easier to solder than original PMC. Rinse thoroughly in water, dry on a soft cloth and repolish as needed.

Press the shard into place in the pendant so it sits all the way down into the bezel. If the underside of the shard is irregular, sprinkle some wood shavings into the bezel. Use a blunt tool to press the walls of the bezel onto the shard. This could be a piece of wooden dowel, a toothbrush handle (cut away the bristle section), or even a plastic pen.

Shadow Box Pendant

Roll out a sheet of PMC to the thickness of a nickel (6 cards, 2 mm). With a ruler and knife, cut way the edges to make a neat square. A credit card makes a handy right-angle template.

Set a ruler or credit card parallel to an edge and about 3/16" (5 mm) in and press it about halfway through the slab. Repeat this process for each edge, then cut away and remove the small squares at each corner.

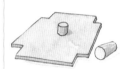

Roll out a thick rod of PMC (about 1/4", 6 mm) and trim one end to make it flat. Cut a length equal to the height of the box walls. Moisten one end with water and press it into the center of the square.

Roll out a long narrow sheet of PMC and cut two strips about 3/16" (4 mm) wide and about three inches long (7 cm). These will be used to make the concentric rings in the center of the pendant. Roll a strip into a ring, slice off the excess and close the joint by pressing the ends together. Moisten the lower edges of this smaller ring and set it into place, pressing down to make a joint. Repeat to make a larger band and attach it to the base.

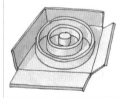

Moisten the edges at each corner of the square and fold the sides up until the ends meet to form a box. This can be done with fingers alone, or by using a blade or card like a spatula to lift the sides. Use your fingernail or a burnishing tool to seal and smooth each corner.

To make the bail, press two small balls of PMC onto the top edge, flattening them into disks. Roll out a rod of PMC about 1/16" thick, form a loop and press the arch-shaped rod onto the disks. Note that the pendant has been placed upside down and a coin is used to hold the loop level. To reinforce this important joint, pick up a tiny bit of PMC on the end of any pointed tool, dampen it and press it gingerly against the place where the rod connects to the pendant.

Dry the piece and fire it as recommended.

After firing and cooling, darken the pendant if desired by following the directions on page 99. Rub the pendant face down on sandpaper to make the edges perfectly uniform. To make the edges shine, rub them with a smooth steel burnisher.

Pendant with Cookie Cutter Overlay

Kitchen stores and candy supply companies offer a wide variety of cookie, petit four and canapé cutters. To make your own cutter, follow the directions on page 114. This project illustrates how you can use the cutter for a basic shape that is then decorated with additional tooling.

Select a cookie cutter and decide on the best overall shape for the pendant; in this case I'll use an oval. Fold a small piece of paper in half and then in half again. Cut a semi-circle with scissors and unfold the paper to examine the oval, repeating the process as necessary until the oval is in proportion to the cookie cutter. Roll out a sheet of PMC (3-5 cards, 1–2 mm) and cut around the paper pattern with a needle tool.

Roll out a PMC sheet a little bigger than the cookie cutter. Press the cutter into the clay and peel away the excess all around. Lift up the cutout and center it on the oval.

Press it down lightly, either with your fingers or, as shown, with a blunt tool such as a pencil eraser. In this example I'll add a few details like the criss-cross of the pineapple husk, but this step will depend on your design.

Roll out a wire of PMC about 5" long and 1/8" thick and flatten it slightly to create a strap that will thicken and embellish the edge. Press the strap onto the oval at the top and lay it along the edge, overlapping slightly. Moisten the joint with water using a small brush and press the band onto the edge of the pendant. When you've made it all the way around, cut off the excess and seal the joint.

Make a small chisel-shaped tool (or use the edge of a ruler or credit card) to create a pattern.

To make a bail, cut away a rectangular section at the top of the pendant and insert a thick slab of PMC that has been cut to the matching size. Moisten the edges and press all the pieces together. Use a small straw to cut a hole in the panel.

Fire and finish.

Textured Drop

Here's an example of a project that is almost too easy to believe. Even though it's simple and quick, the result is an attactive earring that combines elegance with wearability.

Roll out a slab of PMC about as thick as a dime (4 cards, 1.4 mm).

Roll a toothpaste cap along each strip to indent a pattern of parallel lines. The rolling motion will push the strip into a gentle curve. (Tip: If you're using this texture a lot, make a handle of polymer clay to facilitate the rolling action.)

Cut two strips to the same length and gently flip them over so the textured side faces down.

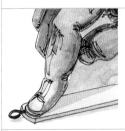

Press a wire loop onto the top of each strip and anchor it by pressing a small ball of PMC on top. Use sterling for PMC+ or PMC 3 and fire them at temperatures below 1500° F. For original PMC, which must be fired at 1650° F, use loops made from fine silver wire. For an alternate design, drill a hole in the top of each strip.

Fire and polish as usual. Thread earwires through the eyelets.

Pie Wedge Earrings

This project uses a simple compass — the kind that draws circles, not the kind that points north — and has the added benefit of making six pieces at once. If you only want one pair of earrings, select your two favorite segments and roll up the remaining PMC for another project.

Make a ball of PMC about the size of a large grape. Holding the lump cupped in your palms, press it to make a disk that is a little thicker in the center than at the edge. The center is thicker than a nickel while the edge can be thinner than a dime.

Set the opening of a compass or dividers (the first has a pencil, the other one doesn't) to a space that looks about half as wide as the PMC disk. Set one leg of the compass in the center and draw a circle, pressing down until you cut all the way through.

Divide the disk into six equal segments by using this setting to "walk" the compass around the circumference. Make a small mark at each place the points touch; these will be used later to determine the sections.

Close the compass and drag decorative circles and arcs through the PMC. These can be deep or shallow, continuous or sporadic, evenly spaced or irregular. These lines can be the only decoration, or you can add to them with stamping, overlay or textures.

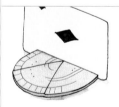

Use a kitchen knife, a tissue blade or a playing card to cut the disk into wedges. Set the straight edge so it touches two of the marks made earlier and passes through the center. Separate the pieces and, if appropriate, select your favorite two.

Cut a small scallop at the top by pressing a drinking straw through the tip of a wedge. Roll a small bit of PMC into a sphere about the size of a peppercorn. Moisten the scallop, set the sphere into place and flatten it with the end of a pen or a pencil. Use a beverage stirrer or a needle tool to poke a hole in the center of this flattened disk.

Fire as usual. After polishing, the earrings can be oxidized to make the lines more dramatic. Insert earwires through the loops.

Small Button

Often the simplest designs are the most effective. This small earring takes advantage of the ability of silver clay to press into itself. Even a simple construction like this layering of three shapes becomes interesting!

Roll out a sheet of PMC about as thick as a dime (4 cards, 1.4 mm). Cut out two squares that are a 1/2" (12 mm) on each side.

Cut two circles a little smaller (3/8", 9 mm) and two more squares that are smaller still. If the clay has started to dry, add a drop of water in the center of the larger square and the circle. Layer the pieces together, centering them.

Press straight down with a ruler, blade or similar flat tool to create decorative lines.

Add the small squares, either by sliding them off the tip of a blade or with a brush.

Press down on the stack to force them together.

Fire as recommended. Polish; darken if desired. Attach earring posts with a small bit of epoxy or solder.

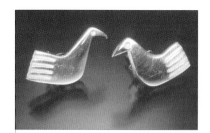

Stylized Bird

Here's a simple earring that illustrates a process you can also use for pins, tie tacs and lots of other projects. For simple images, check out children's books and folk art collections.

Cut the shape from a piece of stiff paper. A playing card works well because of its plastic coating.

Roll out a sheet of PMC about as thick as a nickel (6 cards, 2 mm).

Set the template onto the sheet and roll over it lightly. This will give a faint image of the cutout that makes it easy to create matching parts.

Cut around the shape with a blade. Use a needle tool to reach details.

Add a dot for the eye and use a card to press lines into the tail.

Fire and polish as usual, then solder or glue an earring post onto the back.

Lace Hoop

Here is an earring that takes advantage of the ability of PMC to pick up delicate textures. This example uses lace purchased at a fabric store, but dozens of other textures could be used in the same way.

Roll out a sheet of PMC about as thick as a dime (4 cards, 1.4 mm). Lay a piece of lace onto the sheet and roll over it lightly. Peel off the lace and repeat to make two similar pieces.

Cut away the extra to leave a long oval shape. Repeat to make two.

Flip the pieces over and attach a small piece of PMC at one end. This will create a thick area where you will attach the earring post.

Fire flat at the recommended time and temperature.

After firing, refine the edges with sandpaper and a burnisher.

Glue or solder earring posts. To hang properly in the ear, the post should be angled slightly. Use a few coins to hold the post into position during this process.

Oxidize and polish, then bend each earring into a loop, leaving a gap of about one-quarter of the circle.

Christmas Tree

There are plenty of holidays each year and they all offer possibilities for seasonal jewelry. In addition to illustrating a piece of holiday jewelry, this project shows how simple it can be to create a familiar form. Note, too, the unusual use of a permanent marker in the last step.

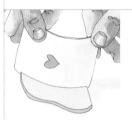

Roll out a slab of PMC about 4 or 5 cards thick (1/8", 1.8 mm).

From this, cut a pair of triangles of equal size. Cut two small rectangles from the bottom edge of each triangle to create the tree trunks.

Use the end of a ruler or tissue blade to press a series of lines along one edge. Don't be surprised when this causes the tree to bend.

Press similar lines along the other side and you'll see the tree straighten.

Add additional lines that crisscross the first set; this will make the texture more complex.

To make a loop for hanging the earring, add a small ball of PMC at the top, press it down and poke a hole in it.

To make ornaments, press into the PMC with a curved tool like the rounded end of a paint brush. Twist the brush to make a smooth crater.

Fire as recommended.

Polish with steel wool, a brass brush or by tumbling. Use a permanent marker to paint the ornaments. This example uses black but colored inks also look great.

Carved Panel

This pair of panel earrings demonstrates a process of carving lines into semi-hard PMC. The pattern here is geometric and symmetrical, but the same technique can be used to create images, text and random marks. Experiment with cutters of various sizes, combining them as needed to create interesting effects. And as a bonus, the process creates small curled shavings of dry PMC that can be layered onto other work for interesting textures.

Roll out a sheet of PMC about the thickness of a dime (4 cards, 1.4 mm). Use a ruler to cut out two matching rectangles. Cut a curve along one of the short sides.

Cut a hole in the center of this edge with a beverage straw or similar tool.

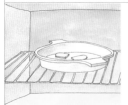

Set the pieces in a glass pie plate or on a steel cookie sheet — no aluminum! — and bake them in a slow oven (250-300° F) for 15-20 minutes. This will drive off the water and create a leather-hard material. Allow the pieces to air cool, which should take only a few minutes.

Draw guidelines in pencil, but don't try to draw every line you intend to cut. Too many pencil lines just make it confusing.

Cut lines with a linoleum block carving tool (available through most art supply stores and from several of the suppliers listed in the appendix).

Cut with a relaxed siding stroke. The PMC should slice like cheese. If the carving is more difficult, sharpen the cutter on fine sandpaper. If you cut a line you don't want, "erase" it by pressing fresh PMC into the groove.

Fire as usual. To complete the earrings, smooth the edges with sandpaper, burnish and darken if desired. Attach a silver earwire.

Split Hoop

These simple, versatile earrings are very easy to make. In this example they hang from a silvewire, but the same split shape can also be constructed like the hoop on page 25. Changing the diameter of the earring will create a very different feeling, from theatrical to understated. The length of the strip before bending will be about three times the diameter of the finished loop.

Select a straight craft (popsicle) stick and sand one edge to make it crisp-edged and smooth.

Roll out a sheet of PMC as thick as a nickel (6 cards, 2 mm).

Tilt the craft stick and press the edge into the sheet to make a uniform groove. Repeat to make at least five parallel grooves.

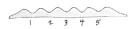

Slide a knife along the first, third and fifth grooves, cutting all the way through. Remove the extra from the sides and trim the length to the desired size. Rule of thumb: a pre-fired length is about 4 times the final diameter, so a strip four inches long now will make a hoop with a 1" diameter.

Separate the two two-strand earring strips. Slice down the center of each strip, starting and ending about 3/8" (9 mm) from the ends. Pull the strands apart a little — final adjustment of the form will be made after firing.

Fire flat at the recommended temperature.

Drill a small hole in each end, then polish to the desired finish. Bend around a convenient cylinder (handle, marker, plastic pipe).

Attach a sterling earwire.

Overlay Ring

Whether you work in PMC or conventional metal, sizing rings is challenging. People's fingers are different sizes and change size throughout the day. Rings that are too tight are uncomfortable and rings that are loose are at risk of falling off. See page 86 for instructions on different ways to achieve a correct size. Each method works and can be used on almost any style of ring. Try them all to determine your favorite.

Determine the proper ring length by wrapping a strip of thick paper around the finger for which you are making the PMC ring. The arithmetic that follows is easiest if you use millimeters. In this example I'll use a size 6, which will require a strip of material that is 54.6 mm long. To allow for shrinkage, the PMC ring needs to be made 28% longer, so I will multiply this figure by 1.28 to yield a figure of 79.9. This is the length I need to make the PMC in order to create a size 6 ring. If your head hurts from the math, refer to the chart on page 86.

Roll a sheet of PMC that will be the bottom layer of the ring.

Roll out a second sheet of PMC a little thinner than the first and cut shapes from it. Roll a toothpaste cap across these pieces to create a selection of textures. Cut these into interesting shapes and press them into place on the band. Add a drop of water at the edge of the overlay; it will be drawn into the layers to confirm the joint.

Cut one end of the ring strap with a knife to make a clean edge. Measure to determine the correct size and cut off the extra material. Squeeze the ends together to seal them. It's often helpful to slide the ring onto a cylinder of some sort (e.g. a dowel, glue stick or marker) to provide support for sealing this joint.

Add another piece of overlay (or modify what's there) to disguise the joint. Set the ring on edge and make it as round as you can by coaxing it with your fingers. Don't worry if it's not perfectly round — this can be adjusted later.

Place the ring on a layer of alumina hydrate or vermiculite and fire it. The layer of powder allows the ring to slide as it shrinks. Though not essential, you can carve a disk from plaster to stop the shrinkage at the correct size. After sintering, slide the ring onto a steel or wooden mandrel and tap it lightly to make it smooth and round.

Found Texture

Jewelry and sentiment are closely linked and always have been. This ring uses actual textures and can have symbolic meaning for the wearer. Imagine capturing the texture of the weathered wood from the family cottage or the boulder you sit on at your special picnic spot....

Use a two-part rubber mold compound to capture the impression of your chosen texture. Here I'm using a weathered board, but the possibilities are endless. Follow the manufacturer's instructions, typically blending equal portions of a putty-like material. Curing time varies between products but is typically between 10 and 45 minutes.

Roll a generous lump of PMC between oiled hands and press it into the mold. Use a rolling pin to create an even pressure as you push the PMC against the rubber mold. Peel the clay off the mold. Determine the pre-fired length needed for the intended size, (chart on page 86) and cut a strip of this length.

Bend the strip of PMC around a cylinder that will make it easy to close the seam. This can be a plastic pipe, a marker, a file handle, test tube, etc. Press the mold over the joint to camouflage the seam if needed.

To halt shrinkage at exactly the right size, rings should be fired over a core made of plaster or a similar heatproof material. Create this by carving the shape from a piece of dried plaster or through the use of a mold. The plaster must be completely dry before it goes into the kiln — make the core several days in advance if possible.

Set the ring on a layer of alumina hydrate or vermiculite with the core in the center and fire as usual. After firing the ring can be quenched in water (assuming there are no stones), which will cause the plaster to crack apart. If allowed to air dry, break the plaster out with a pointed tool.

Oxidize, sand the edges and polish to best display the texture.

Ring with Gold Ornaments

Gold PMC fires at a higher temperature than silver PMC, so care must be taken when combining them. In this case, the silver ring shank provides the strength of the piece, so even though the gold is underfired, the ring will be durable. This ring adds the allure and value of gold at a relatively low cost since the gold is a small part of the whole piece.

Roll out a slab of PMC of the intended thickness. This will depend on the size and design of the ring, but will probably be around 3-6 cards thick. Cut a strip to make the shank, beveling or rolling the edges in the process.
Cut to the proper length for the ring size.

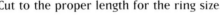

Moisten each location with a drop of water. Make a small dent with a pencil point or rubber-tipped modeling tool at the intended location for each gold ornament.

Pinch off a small piece of 24K PMC and set it into place, pressing with a tool. In this example I've carved lines into the end of an 1/8" dowel.

Allow to dry, then fire as recommended. In this example a disk of plaster is being used to hold the ring to a desired size, but this is only one
option. See page 86 for more about ring sizing.

Twice-Fired Ring

One of the great things about PMC is that it can be fired more than once. This means that elements can be added, repaired and changed as a piece develops. This project shows how the two-step process can be used to size a ring.

Roll out a sheet of silver clay (I prefer PMC+ or PMC3 for rings) at least 4 cards thick, (3/16", 1.4 mm). Mark three parallel lines by lightly pressing a card or ruler into the clay. Hold a block of wood or plastic so its corner meets the PMC at a 45° angle. Press it at least halfway into the sheet. Repeat equally on all three lines.

Cut the shank to length and slice along the two outer grooves, removing the clay on either side. The purpose of these grooves is to give shape to the outer edges of the band.

Cut the groove all the way through on the last half inch (12 mm) of the shank. Before you lift the blade, swing it left and right to pull the two legs of the ring outward.

Pinch off two small bits of PMC and roll them into small balls. Set these at the notches of the "V" on each end of the ring shank and press them with a tool (pencil, stamp, toothpick, etc.) to both flatten and ornament. Set the shank aside to dry.

Make an ornament for the top of the ring. Here I'm using the flower demonstrated on page 15, but the possibilities are endless. However you do it, mold, build or texture this piece and allow it to dry.

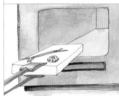

Fire both pieces, the shank and the central ornament. After quenching or cooling, refine both shapes as needed with files, sandpaper, etc. Do not polish or oxidize yet.

 Bend the shank around a convenient cylinder (pipe, marker, broomstick, etc.) and adjust it to the correct size. File the top ends of the shank as needed to make them uniform and close to the finger.

 Press a lump of PMC+ or PMC 3 onto the back of the flower and squeeze it onto the shank, blending with tools and a moistened finger to make a smooth transition. Make the lump a little oversized, remembering that it will shrink.

 Set the ring on a mound of alumina hydrate or vermiculite and fire again. Because the fresh PMC is bonding with already-fired solid metal, allow extra time for the bond to secure. For PMC+ or PMC 3, fire at least one hour. Finish as usual.

Single Stone

There are about a million ways to set a gem in PMC. This project shows one — the setting is created as a separate, geometric unit then attached to a shank. Other possibilities would integrate the stone into the shank.

Press out a thick patty of PMC and cut a hole in the center. For the rectangular stone in this example, I've cut two plugs to better match the shape of the gem. Press the stone into the hole, deep enough that the top surface is below the level of the surrounding PMC.

Cut away the excess with a blade or playing card to create an attractive setting.

To make a double-band shank, either follow the directions for the Double Fired Ring on the preceding pages or try this alternative. Roll out a thick rod of PMC or PMC+ or PMC3 and slice it in half lengthwise with a knife or playing card.

Roll out a thin sheet of PMC, dampen it slightly and press the half-round rods onto this base. Trim away the excess, then cut this strip to a length that will not quite go around your finger after firing. You can determine this by using the chart on page 86.

Bend the shank around a ring mandrel or rod and trim to create a gap in the shank that will accept the setting. Fill the space with PMC+ or PMC3 paste. For more information about gemstones and how to use them, see pages 92 and 93.

Set the dried band on a layer of alumina hydrate or vermiculite and fire as recommended. Allow the gem to cool slowly.

Carved Geometric Ring

We usually associate PMC with rich textures and organic forms. Here's a ring that illustrates the exciting options for highly refined planar forms. This ring, more than any other shown here, is typical of a design that could be carved in wax and cast through the centrifugal process. Casting is a valuable process for those equipped for the technique. For the rest, PMC offers a convenient alternative.

Determine your ring size as described on page 86. Use the chart on that page to decide on the appropriate length of the shank before firing. I recommend PMC+ or PMC3 for rings because of its increased strength, but standard PMC can also be used for this ring.

Wind electrical tape around a dowel or marker until the diameter comes up to the intended ring size. Wrap the mandrel with Saran or waxed paper to keep the ring from sticking.

Roll out a thick strip (8 cards, 3 mm) of any version of PMC. Don't be skimpy here — the more material you have, the more dramatic your carving can be. Bend the strip around the sizing stick, cut the ends on a slope and press them together to form a solid joint.

Allow the ring to harden for a few minutes so you can slide it off the mandrel without distorting it, then set the ring aside in a way that air can reach all sides evenly.

After at least two hours (overnight is better) set the ring on a glass or steel cooking pan and place it in a warm oven (325°) for at least 15 minutes to drive off whatever moisture remains.

Divide the ring into four equal parts with pencil lines.

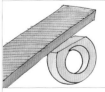

File to create the desired form, catching the PMC dust for recycling. When the shape is correct, switch to sandpaper to further refine and smooth the ring.

Fire as recommended.

Use polishing papers and/or mechanical polishing to finish the ring.

Band Ring with Gemstones

This project uses a tool called a firing mandrel that can be purchased from suppliers listed at the back of the book. This tool contains the finished diameter on its smaller end and a calculated pre-fired size for rings made from standard PMC. Rings can also be made over a plaster plug (see page 31) or without any internal support.

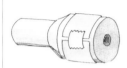

A firing mandrel is a short rod of refractory material (i.e., something that withstands heat) that has two specific diameters. The smaller half of each rod equals standard ring sizes. To prevent sticking, start by wrapping a strip of waxed paper around the larger end. Secure it with tape.

Roll out a thick rod of PMC and slice it in half lengthwise to make a half round wire. Wrap it around the paper-covered form, cut to length and seal the joint by smearing the ends into one another. In this example I'll make a narrow band with a line of stones, but any sort of ring can be made on the mandrel.

Make pencil guidelines on the top of the mandrel, dividing it into eight equal sections. This will guide placement of the gems.

Poke a hole for each stone with a pencil point and cut away a bit of PMC with a beverage stirrer or a needle tool.

Press a gem into each hole until it is at least one millimeter below the surface. Use a flat topped rod (like a pen top or lollipop stick) to press the stones into place. Allow the ring to dry for at least half an hour; this will make it stiff enough to slide off the firing mandrel without being distorted.

Pull off and discard the waxed paper. Set the ring on a low pile of alumina hydrate or vermiculite on a tile that will go into the kiln. Wrap the small end of the mandrel with a strip of ceramic paper and seal it with tape. This paper will not burn away in the firing process and will prevent the ring from sticking to the mandrel.

Place the mandrel, small end down, into the ring. Fire as usual. The PMC will shrink until it touches the plug. Because it cannot shrink any further, it will "redirect" whatever shrinking remains into a barely perceptible thinning.

After air cooling the ring, pull it off the firing mandrel and closely examine each setting. Use a small burnisher (a scribe, nail set or dental tool) to press the PMC neatly over each stone. This will make a brightly polished frame to highlight the stones.

Leaf Bead

This project is about as simple as a bead can get. In addition to celebrating the wonderful textures that surround us, this project demonstrates how the combustibility of materials can be used to simplify work in PMC. You'll have a dozen made before you realize it!

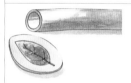

Roll out a thin slab of PMC, about as thick as a dime (4 cards, 1.4 mm). Set a green leaf, face up, onto the slab and roll again to press its texture into the clay. Cut around the leaf with a knife or needle.

Cut the lower third off the PMC leaf and press it slightly with the roller. The intention here is to create a thin edge where the layers overlap.

Lift the leaf off, or, alternately, leave it in place. When the PMC is fired the leaf will burn away harmlessly.

Roll the PMC around a drinking staw, pencil or other handy form. Moisten the ends and press them lightly together to close the bead.

Fire the beads by placing them on a bed of alumina hydrate or vermiculite.

Oxidize and polish as desired.

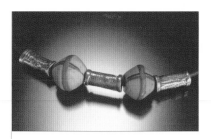

Tube Bead

Here's a great idea that works in just about any size, either all by itself, in multiples, or as a spacer between stone, glass or polymer beads. In this example the bead is formed over a plastic drinking straw, but a rolled-up tube of paper can also be used.

Roll out a slab of PMC about as thick as a dime (4 cards, 1.4 mm) and cut a straight edge along one side with a sharp knife. We'll call this the joint edge. Cut two edges perpendicular to this edge; these will determine the length of the bead. Press a roller on the joint edge to thin it slightly. This will allow for a strong overlapping joint.

Texture the slab in any of, oh, a gazillion ways. In this example I'm going to drag a comb across the surface, but you could also press any material into the clay or imprint it with tools or rubber stamps. Flip the piece over so the textured side faces down.

Cut off a piece of a drinking straw (paper or plastic) a little bit longer than your bead. Roll the slab over the straw, starting with the joint edge. Use a knife or the edge of a playing card to cut a clean line at the leading edge of the joint. Press the PMC down on itself, pulling it slightly as needed to create an overlap. Seal the joint by rubbing it with a fingernail or a modeling tool.

Roll out another slab of PMC, this one a little thicker than the first. Cut off two strips that will be used at each end of the bead. This will make the bead stronger and simultaneously provide contrast between the darkened texture and the smooth raised molding. Dampen the ends of the PMC tube with water and wrap the strips around, joining them as you did the tube.

Allow the bead to dry, then pull out the straw. It could be allowed to burn up during firing, but removing it now prevents the unpleasant odor of burning plastic. Set the beads into a kiln on a small pile of alumina hydrate or vermiculite. If many beads are being fired at the same time, use a dish to hold the powder as described on page 95. Fire as usual. In this example the bead has been tumbled, darkened, then polished with a rouge cloth.

Disk Bead

Large or small, plain or fancy, you'll use this bead with gem or polymer clay spacers in a necklace, as a component in earrings or on a cord all by itself. Use your imagination to expand on the possibilities presented here.

Pull off an almond-size piece of PMC and roll it into a sphere between your palms.

Poke a small straw or skewer through the center of the sphere. This should be only a couple of inches long so it doesn't get in your way in the next step.

Move around the outer edge of the disk, pinching it repeatedly between your thumb and finger. The idea is to create a disk that is thick in the center and thin at the edge.

Add subtle decoration by rolling a tube cap into the bead.

Place the bead on a small mound of alumina hydrate or vermiculite on a tile or directly on the floor of the kiln. Fire as recommended. Tumble or burnish by hand. In the latter case, experiment with burnishing only selected areas to exaggerate the design.

Cylinder with Spiral Wrap

This project shows how to use a special consistency of PMC+ and PMC 3 that is loaded in a syringe. Standard PMC can be used in the same way, but usually requires some kind of help to be pushed through the device. For more information on the extruding process, see page 82. Instructions for making your own extruder can be found on page 116.

Make a cylinder bead over a core of some material that will burn away completely. This could be papier-maché, paper, Styrofoam or a drinking straw.

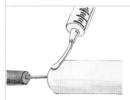

Slide a needle tool (or toothpick, skewer, etc.) into one end, stopping before it pokes out the other side. This handle will make it easier to rotate the bead.

A specially-formulated extrudable PMC is available already loaded into plastic syringes. Hold a syringe near the end of a bead and squirt out a thread of PMC about a half an inch long. Press it lightly onto the cylinder to make it stick. Rotate the bead as you squeeze out more PMC, trying for equal spacing between coils. To make a thinner line, pull the PMC thread slightly as you proceed.

If the thread snaps, overlap slightly and continue. Leave the joint alone for now — it can be smoothed with a dampened brush later.

After the beads have dried, set them onto a pile of alumina hydrate or vermiculite and fire as usual.

Raku Donut Beads

Here's an unusual surface treatment that is commonly associated with ceramics. The process starts with a PMC bead made in the usual way. The bead is then painted with a special glaze that is fused onto the silver. Even more than most projects, experimentation is a necessary part of this exciting and unpredictable process.

Carve or mold a core from a totally combustible material.

Roll out a sheet of PMC about 4 cards thick (1/16", 1.4 mm) and mark out a circle with a compass or dividers. Make the clay circle a little larger than the core. Make two pieces — one for the top and one for the bottom of the bead.

Dampen the edges and center, then sandwich the core between the two disks of PMC, pinching the two sheets together. Press down in the center until the sheets are bonded, then cut away the clay in the center of the donut. Smooth the edges and even out the surface.

Allow the piece to dry, then fire as recommended. Set the bead on a pile of alumina hydrate, vermiculite, or plaster powder to support it throughout the firing process. When the bead has cooled, the surface can be sanded, burnished or scratchbrushed to prepare it for the raku glaze.

Raku glazes are usually sold as a powder and are available from ceramic supply companies. The example shown is called Tutti Frutti and is available from Laguna Clay Company, www.lagunaclay.com (800-4524-4862). Mix with water to a milky consistency, stirring well. Dip the bead into the glaze to create an even coating. The thickness of this layer will determine whether the coating is a crusty green or a thin bronzy patina.

To keep the glazed surface from touching anything, make a hanging hook from coat hanger wire. Hang the bead and allow the glaze to dry for several minutes. Put the bead into a kiln and bring it up to the temperature needed to melt the glaze. Usually it takes only a few minutes to heat the glaze into a syrupy consistency.

Fill a metal container (e.g. a soup can) with a combustible material — sawdust, pine needles, pencil shavings, or leaves. Place the container on a cookie sheet or other non-flammable surface.

When the surface appears uniformly wet and shiny, pull the bead from the kiln and quickly drop it into the can. Cover with a tile or brick to capture the smoke. Allow the piece to cool in the smoldering wood, then take it out and rub it vigorously to remove soot, loose glaze and bits of wood. During this process, protect your hands and arms by wearing gloves and a long-sleeved shirt.

The bead can be used as is or finished with a brass brush or steel wool.

Cylinder Bead with Polymer Clay

Precious Metal Clay and polymer clay are modeled and worked in similar ways and with similar tools. The two modern materials are easy partners. One brings value, luster, durability and heft, while the other contributes color, translucency and delicate transitions. Together they can be used for everything from earrings to watch fobs. This project illustrates a single approach but points the way to dozens of other possibilities.

The first step is to make a bead of PMC with spaces to be filled with polymer clay. The metal piece will be fired and polished before the polymer clay is added. Make a core of any material that can be easily burned away. For this bead I rolled up a tube of paper and held it closed with tape.

Roll out a sheet of PMC as thick as a dime (4 cards, 1.4 mm) and cut off two adjoining edges to make an accurate right angle. Decide on the length of the bead and cut a strip this wide. Lay one end of the strip onto the paper tube and roll it over the PMC as if you were rolling up a miniature carpet. When you feel the "bump" of the first edge, unroll slightly. You will see a faint mark in the PMC that will indicate where the sheet needs to be cut. Moisten the seam, overlap the edges and smooth the joint until it disappears.

Roll out a slightly thicker slab of PMC to make bands that wrap around the bead. The thickness of these pieces (after firing) will determine the thickness of the polymer clay. Add a cap at each end, trimming off some of the paper roll if necessary.

Allow the bead to dry, then fire it on a small mound of alumina hydrate or vermiculite. Finish the bead by burnishing, tumbling or scratchbrushing. Rinse the bead thoroughly to remove any soap residue and allow it to dry completely.

Condition the polymer clay, layering and blending to create whatever color or image you want. Paint the recessed section of the bead with SOBO, acrylic medium or a similar plastic glue and allow it to dry for a minute or two. Press the polymer onto the bead and close the joint by rubbing the edges together. Cure the polymer in an oven according to the manufacturer's directions. This relatively low heat will not affect the PMC.

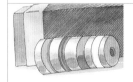

After the bead has cooled, use sandpapers of decreasing grit to make the surface flush and smooth. At 600 grit the silver will be bright and the polymer will have a pleasant luster. To make the PMC shinier, use microgrit polishing papers or steel wool.

Spherical Bead

This project demonstrates a hollow object and the use of simple overlays as ornaments. In this example, decorative elements are shaped as they are being placed on the bead, a variation with a lot of room for further development.

Make a core from a combustible material like paper pulp or bread. Styrofoam can be used if the firing process will take place away from people in a ventilated room. Mount the core on a toothpick or skewer to make it easy to handle.

Roll out a sheet of PMC about 3 cards (1 mm) thick, then use it to wrap the sphere in an even layer of PMC. One way to accomplish this is to cut two disks of PMC, then press them onto opposite ends of the sphere — think north pole and south pole. Cut a rectangular belt and wrap this around the equator of the sphere and seal all seams. Finish by rolling the bead lightly in your palms to make the surface even. Do not press too hard or the PMC layer will stretch.

Cut a hole for the bead cord, relocate the toothpick handle here and cut a similar hole opposite from the first.

Cut disks from a sheet of PMC with a straw or beverage stirrer. Dampen the intended site and press each piece into place.

To make an ornamental plus sign (✚), press a square tool (edge of a ruler, etc.) in each of four quadrants of a disk. With a little practice you'll find that a press-and-slide action will make a seamless joint. To make ornamental circles, press on a disk as before and moisten it to make sure it is pliable. Push the end of a paintbrush or any similar pointed tool into the disc to make a crater in the center. After firing, sand the top rim to reveal a decorative circle.

Press a needle or sharp pencil into the bead to make a subtle pattern on the surface of the bead.

Lay the bead on a bed of alumina hydrate or vermiculite and fire as usual.

Thumbprint Tie Tac

This piece is as easy as it is special — a great gift for a dad, uncle or grandfather. Use your own thumbprint or someone else's. With a few changes you can use this idea for earrings, a ring or as bracelet links.

Put a drop of olive oil in your palm and spread it over your hands.

Pull off a piece of PMC about the size of a peanut. Roll it into an oval ball and set it in the palm of one hand.

Press a thumb onto the lump, squeezing it to a flattened pad. Open the palm holding the lump and allow it to drop to the table. Poke a shallow hole in the back with a toothpick and let it dry for at least 10 minutes.

The semihardened thumbprint can now be handled without danger of smearing the print. Use an emery board or piece of sandpaper to flatten and smooth the back of the piece (the surface that was against the palm). You might want to scratch a name and date onto the back with a pin.

Fire as recommended. Solder a tie tack pin into the hole and the piece is done.

Variation:
To make beads, roll the PMC around a core of string, broom straw, or monofilament fishing line. Pinch the lump to make a fingerprint or thumbprint on two sides and fire as usual. After firing, string the beads onto a cord, perhaps using glass or gemstone beads as spacers.

Alternately, use sterling wire as described on page 104 to make each print a separate bead.

Cuff Link from a Button Mold

This project uses a two-part rubber mold material that was also used in the ring on page 32. Moldmaking opens rich and varied possibilities, not only for matching objects like these cuff links, but for appliqués, repeating links and production items. Mold materials can be found at art supply stores or through mail-order companies. Check the list of suppliers at the end of the book for sources.

Select a button that is a bit larger than the desired cuff link.

Mix equal parts of the mold putty until the color is homogenous and forms a thick, flat lump. Press the button into the mold until it is just even with the surface. Set aside to cure, usually 10-30 minutes. Test by pressing the rubber with a fingernail. When it bounces back without making a mark, the mold has set. Pop the button out.

Roll a lump of PMC between oiled palms to lubricate its outer surface. Press or roll the clay into the mold, pull it out and set aside to dry. Repeat.

Roll out a rod of PMC about 1/8" (3 mm) thick. Also roll out a thick sheet and cut two squares to become the back caps of the cuff links. Press a 1/2" section of rod onto the center of each square.

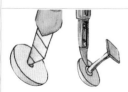

When the button units are dry enough to handle (10-15 minutes), carve a small hole in the back of each one. Moisten, set a bit of PMC into the socket and press the rod and back cap snugly into place. Allow to dry.

Lay the cuff links on their sides on a bed of vermiculite or alumina hydrate and fire as usual.

Finish by oxidizing and polishing with steel wool, a brass brush or a nylon pad.

Charms

Charms are often hung in a collection on a bracelet, but they can be used singly or in small groups as pendants and watchband accessories. Charms are usually tokens of a person's interests, hobbies or profession. These examples crack open the door to a huge room of possibilities.

Coffee Mug
Create a form from Styrofoam, polymer clay or light wood. Wrap a sheet of PMC around it and seal the joint. Cut a disk of the same sheet and attach it onto the end to make the bottom of the mug.

Roll a thick piece of PMC, cut a hole with a beverage stirrer, then trim around the hole to make a handle for the mug. Spread a generous layer of slip onto one edge and press this against the mug. Smooth the soft PMC with a brush to make a smooth transition between the parts.

Add a loop for hanging. I've placed it beneath the handle, but other locations would also work. This looks a little odd at this stage, but this loop will be less obvious when the charm in hung on a bracelet.

Open Book
Cut and trim two thin slabs of PMC to be the cover of the book. Lay these over a narrow strip that represents the spine.

Roll out a thick sheet of PMC, then press it with a roller to make the shape of the open pages. Cut in half to create two identical pieces. Lay these onto the covers and press the edges with a blade to simulate the edges of the pages.

Cut a curved section away from the top edge to make a seat for the loop. Dampen this area and press a loop of PMC into place there. Reinforce it with slip.

Squash Racket

Roll out a thick sheet of PMC for the handle and cut a narrow strip from it. Make a cut about a half inch in, centered on the shaft, then pull the two legs outward to make a "Y" shape.

To make the stringed section, roll out a thin sheet and press a card or blade into it, first one way and then perpendicular to that, to represent the webbing. Cut out an oval, either freehand or using a template.

Cut a thin strip of PMC and wrap it around the oval, adding a drop of water to secure the joint.

Join the two sections, using water or slip to facilitate the joint. Cut a scallop in the end of the handle and press a small sphere of PMC into place there. Flatten it and insert a needle tool, wiggling it slightly to make a hole for hanging.

Animal Cracker Barrette

This project shows how something as simple as a cookie can be used to create a form. Besides animal crackers, you might get ideas by cutting photos from magazines, cutting into wallpaper, or taking patterns from other crafts such as embroidery, stenciling and rubber stamping.

Buy a box of animal crackers (tell the clerk they're for your niece...). Eat one or two.

Choose your favorite creature and study how it is made. The cookie dough loses definition as it bakes, so you'll be able to improve on the forms you see.

Roll out a slab of PMC about as thick as a nickel (6 cards, 2 mm). Trace your cracker onto it with a needle or sharp pencil.

Lift the cookie away — don't eat it yet — and cut out the shape. Do this with a knife, or by going around the outline several times with a needle.

Use a pencil eraser or similar blunt modeling tool to press areas down as needed to create legs, eyes and other details. With the tool held at an angle, press down the edges to make them rounded. Allow your "cookie" to dry for at least 10 minutes (overnight is okay).

Use sandpaper or emery boards on the dry PMC to round the edges and refine the form.

Fire and polish as usual.

Use epoxy to glue a barrette finding onto the back.

Oval Barrette with Granular Texture

The dramatic texture used in this piece has scores of other uses. Besides the decorative potential, the method described in the first step is also a time-saving shortcut for rehydrating dry PMC, described on page 80.

Collect dried scraps or create small pieces of PMC by cutting scraps into pieces about the size of peppercorns (3-4 mm in diameter). Grind the pieces in a pepper mill (or similar hand grinding tool), catching the granules on a piece of paper. To make smaller grains, run the PMC particles through the mill two or three times.

Fold a piece of paper in half, then in half again and cut it to make an oval pattern. Roll out a slab of PMC as thick as a nickel (6 cards, 2 mm) and trace around the oval template with a needle tool.

Set the paper pattern on the oval so that the top section of the PMC base is exposed. Paint a layer of slip on the uncovered area.

Sprinkle granules onto the slip, pressing down slightly to help them bond.

Fire as recommended.

Bend the piece slightly by pressing it over your knee and polish the smooth portion. Blacken to increase the contrast between the polished and textured area.

Attach a commercial barrette finding with epoxy.

Polymer Bracelet with PMC Inserts

In recent years, polymer clay has exploded onto the crafts scene. It's ease of use, bright colors and versatility have earned it an enthusiastic following. Though the material is not difficult to use, using it well deserves more instruction than can be devoted here. People with experience in polymer might see possibilities in this bracelet for exciting ways to combine PMC and polymer. Beginners are encouraged to seek out instructional books on polymer clay or find local workshops.

To make a scarab in PMC, press a lump into a flattened oval, then press a ruler or credit card into the clay to divide it into segments. Add detail texture at the head. Make other embellishments either freehand or by carving the reverse of the desired form into soap as explained in the following project. Allow these pieces to dry and fire them as recommended.

Finish the PMC elements, sanding, burnishing, tumbling and coloring as desired.

Purchase polymer clay, either in the color you want, or in two or three colors that you will combine to make a unique blend. Sculpey III is not recommended for this project because it is not strong enough. Condition the polymer very well. This is important, not only because it makes the clay easier to use, but because proper conditioning insures maximum strength.

Roll out a rod of polymer about 1/2″ (12 mm) in diameter. Flatten it with a rolling pin (or a drinking glass).

Texture the polymer by pressing down on it with a stiff brush or coarse sandpaper.

Lay the bracelet over a curved surface and press the PMC units part way into the plastic band.

Curl the bracelet into its final form and lay it onto a glass pie plate. Press small lumps of polymer as needed to hold the curve intact. It is also useful to roll a strip of paper (joined with tape) to hold the form from the inside.

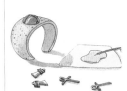

Bake according to manufacturer's directions with the PMC elements in position. Increased curing time translates to a stronger material, so I'd leave this bracelet at 260-275° F for 90 minutes. Set a scrap piece of the same polymer into the pan as a test piece. It can be any size or shape, but it must be the same thickness as the bracelet. After curing and cooling, try to break this scrap in your fingers. If it snaps, return the bracelet to the oven for further curing.

Allow the piece to air cool, then rub it lightly with fine sandpaper, nylon abrasive pads, or steel wool. To enrich the texture, rub acrylic paint into the marks and wipe away excess. Allow the paint to dry.

The PMC pieces might have been adequately trapped in the polymer clay to hold them, but in most cases you'll want to glue them into the bracelet with epoxy (page 103).

Hinged Link Bracelet

This flexible bracelet is made of repeating units that are joined with a hinge-like pivot. The first step is to make a pattern and from that, make a mold. Multiple links are created by pressing PMC into this mold, then they are fired, polished and assembled.

The pattern is made from 1/8" (3 mm) square rod of wood, metal or plastic. Cut three pieces, each 1/2" long. Round the edges slightly with sandpaper.

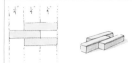

Glue or solder the pieces together so the center piece is projecting 1/4" beyond the outside pieces. Sand this to make it smooth and precise.

Lay the pattern on a flat surface. Mix equal parts of silicone mold putty together, twisting and kneading until the color is uniform. To insure that the mold compound reaches into every corner, start by putting small bits of it into the recesses of the form. Press the rest of the putty over the pattern and down against the table. Make the bottom of the mold (now facing up) parallel to the tabletop by flattening the mold with a board or similar flat object. Allow the mold to cure (usually 15-30 minutes), then remove the pattern.

Roll a small quantity of PMC between oiled palms, then press it into the mold. Flex the mold to pop it out, repeating to make enough links to fit around your wrist. A standard length (6") will require 12. Allow them to dry completely.

Sand or file each link as needed to refine the form.

Drill a hole through both ends of each link (the single and the double arms) with a small drill bit. An electric drill or flexible shaft machine makes this easier, but it can be done by hand.

Test the assembly with a wire that makes a close fit. It might be necessary to re-drill the holes to make them line up. Sand as needed to allow the links to move properly.

To make a catch, modify one of the links to create a hook. Drill a hole across the end of the finger of one link, then use a blade, sawblade or file to cut into the bar until you connect with the hole. Set the link aside to dry. When it is stiff enough to handle, refine the shape with sandpaper. Note that the hook slants backward slightly.

Insert a piece of wire across the two outer fingers of the other end link. If you have made the bracelet of PMC+ or PMC 3, this can be made of sterling and fired in place at the low temperature required by that metal. If using original PMC, use nickle silver or fine silver wire and fire at the full temperature for two hours.

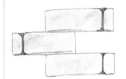

Finish each link separately, polishing or leaving areas matte as suits your design sense. Use a slightly larger drill bit to make a slight bevel at the lip of each hole. Do this by hand — the bit is only rotated once or twice.

To assemble the chain, slide sterling wire through the links and snip it so only a small amount sticks out. File this flat across the end and tap it lightly with a small hammer to make a rivet. This will prevent the wire from slipping out.

Quilt Pattern with Enamel

This bold pin uses a traditional quilt pattern — a design resource with vast potential. The project introduces the use of a constructed mold and shows how enamels can be used on fired PMC.

Draw the pattern on paper or with the help of a computer.

Transfer the design onto a sheet of plastic. Art stores sell a plastic mat board made of PVC (e.g., Celtek) that works very well. Cut pieces for the parts of the design that will be recessed and glue them onto a base. Draw a grid on the base first to help in positioning the pieces.

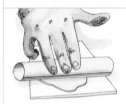

Roll a sheet of PMC over the board to create the design. One of the benefits of this system is that it is easy to make multiples.

Trim off extra material around the edge of the piece. Use the edge of a ruler or blade to add linear details.

Dry and fire as recommended. Polish the piece by burnishing or tumbling to prepare for enameling. Solder a pin finding on the back with Hard (high melting) silver solder. If you prefer to attach the pin back with glue, wait until after the last step.

Wash powdered enamels in clean water and set the polished and cleaned pin into a tripod to support it during firing. Lay each color into place with a fine brush, allow the moisture to evaporate, then fire according to the manufacturer's suggestions. Add more enamel and refire as needed to fill the chambers. This pin uses Thompson transparent enamels: Periwinkle Blue, (2615), Purple (2755) and Woodrow Pink (2880).

Grind the surface flat with abrasive stones working under a trickle of water to flush away debris. To create a shiny surface, refire one last time.

Polish the exposed silver areas with micromesh polishing papers and a rouge cloth.

Petroglyph Pin

Here's a technique that is both easy and versatile. In this pin, an image is carved into a bar of soap, transferred to PMC and layered to frame it.

Scrape the top surface of a bar of hand soap to remove the brand name. Press or carve a design into the soap with a needle, nail, awl, pencil, etc. Experiment with various tools and brands of soap to discover the huge range of possibilities. Remember that the image must be carved in the reverse of the way you want it to appear. Thin deep lines into the mold tend to hold onto the PMC which will damage the design. To allow for better release, cut the lines so they have a "V" shape.

Pull off a ball of PMC and roll it between oiled palms to create a thin film on the surface. Pinch it into a patty and roll the PMC into the soap mold. Peel off and check the design, recarving the soap as needed to make a clean impression.

Trim off excess PMC and set the impression aside.

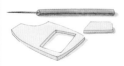

Roll out a slab of PMC 4-6 cards thick (1.4-2 mm) and cut a window to fit the impression. Cut away the edges to make an interesting shape.

Lift the frame and slide the impression into place beneath it, pressing down to lock them together. Trim and smooth the edges as needed.

To make a pendant, add a loop or a hole. In this example the pin finding will be attached later. Fire as usual.

To create a high contrast, the frame piece was given a high shine by sanding it with the full range of abrasive papers, all the way to a high finish micromesh polishing paper.

Cord Ends

Caps for the ends of cords and thongs are commercially available, but here are a few PMC variations that allow you to design work that coordinates with the piece.

Roll up a strip of paper to be the internal form and wrap it with plastic tape. Cut the ends to make them even.

Roll out a thin sheet of PMC, trim to size and wrap the paper form. Seal the joint by adding a drop of water, then smooth the joint with a flat tool.

Roll out a sheet and cut out two circles to make end caps. Moisten the surfaces and press each onto the end of the cylinder. Wet your fingers and rotate the form in a soft grip to seal the seam.

Cut the bead in half with a knife to make two identical parts. After drying, separate the halves and remove the paper core.

Roll out a rod of PMC about 3/32" (3 mm) in diameter and a couple of inches long. Drape this around itself to make a circle and cut. Cut a flat angle at the joint.

Set the loop into place on the end of the cylinder, lifting it on coins as needed. Press the parts together to make a solid joint. It's a good idea to add more material to reinforce the joint. Fire as usual.

Tapered Cap
Roll a triangle of paper and tape it to make a core for this bead. This will probably be removed before firing, but if it becomes stuck inside the bead, the paper will simply burn away.

Cut a triangle from a PMC sheet and wrap it loosely around the paper form. Seal the joints with a dampened finger.

Roll the bead under your fingers, pressing the tip into a solid rod. Dampen the solid end slightly to make it pliable, then curl it back onto itself to make a loop. Press the end down to seal it to the body of the cap.

Fire on a small mound of alumina hydrate or vermiculite and finish as usual.

Monogram Keychain

This project is equally appropriate as a gift for a man or a woman. It can be a first project, but offers challenges to advanced workers too.

Start by drawing designs, either contained in a circle, oval or square, or freeform. I'll use the example of a monogram but, of course, this could as easily be a person's name or a company logo. If the letters are the same size they should be in proper order: John A. Smith = JAS. If the initial of the last name is to be prominent, it is in the center: JSA.

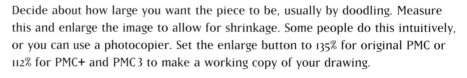

Decide about how large you want the piece to be, usually by doodling. Measure this and enlarge the image to allow for shrinkage. Some people do this intuitively, or you can use a photocopier. Set the enlarge button to 135% for original PMC or 112% for PMC+ and PMC3 to make a working copy of your drawing.

Roll out a slab of PMC at least 1/16" thick (5 cards, 1.6 mm). Set the drawing onto the slab and prick along the lines with a pin to transfer the design.

The monogram will be made into a relief by pressing the background down. Do this with the back end of a pen or the eraser of a new pencil. An eraser can be shaped to give it a sharp edge and a texture if desired. Many other tools can be used for this — look around for simple tools like popsicle sticks, toothpicks, nails and lollipop sticks.

Add a loop for the key ring. Because this area will take a lot of stress it is important to make a solid joint. Roll out a thick slab of PMC, cut out a small disk and poke a hole in the center with a straw. Cut a notch in the edge of the monogram piece, moisten both edges and press the parts together. Turn the piece over and rub the seam to strengthen it. Fire as usual, polish and darken. Attach a commercial key ring with a jump ring.

Simple Buttons

Have you ever made a shirt or dress and been unable to find just the right button? Maybe you've knitted a great sweater or bought a blazer that needs a special touch. Long after the clothes are gone, you can bet these silver buttons will have moved on to new uses!

Consider the sizes you'll need and determine how many of each you want. You might want to make extras. Use the templates below to determine the pre-fired sizes needed for standard button diameters.

Roll out a piece of PMC and cut out the circles you need. You can trace a coin, use a plastic template, or cut them out with a knife. The best way to make identical disks is with a piece of tube that will work like a cookie cutter, as described on page 114.

This pattern was made by rolling a cap in arcing paths across each disk. Other possible textures or ornaments include weathered wood, bicycle reflectors, fingerprints and rubber stamps.

Use a beverage stirrer to cut holes in the buttons. If these are too large for your design, poke holes with a needle. These can be enlarged and made round by drilling or filing after the buttons have been fired.

Fire and polish as usual.

Final Size	Size before firing	
5/8	PMC+ PMC3	PMC
1/2		
3/8		

Theme Buttons

Silver buttons will make any shirt or blazer special. And if those buttons were handmade and personalized for the wearer, the garment would be very special.

Cut off a convenient length of half-inch wooden dowel and round the top with files and sandpaper. Alternatively, you might be able to find the form we are after in a file handle or the end of a broom. Polymer clay workers will probably find it easiest to make a form from that useful material.

Roll out a slab of PMC about as thick as a dime (4 cards, 1.4 mm) and cut out a disk for the button. Standard button sizes and their pre-fired PMC size are shown on page 63. To cut a circle, use a needle to trace around a plastic template or a coin.

Press the disk over the rounded form to create a dome. Ornament as appropriate. To make this golf ball, I used the tip of a knitting needle. To make a baseball, draw a curved line with a needle tool, then touch repeatedly with a razor knife to make the stitches. Allow the piece to dry for about ten minutes, then pull it off the rod.

Rub the disk back and forth on a piece of sandpaper or an emery board to make the edge flat and even.

Roll out a thick slab of PMC, perhaps 3 mm or the thickness of two quarters stacked together. Cut a strip from this that is at least an inch long and 1/8" to 1/4" wide. This will become the tab that allows the button to be sewn on.

Make a hole in the strip near but not right at the tip. Use a small straw to remove a bit of PMC or poke a hole with a needle tool and enlarge by wiggling the tool in the hole.

Dampen the end of the strip and press it firmly into the button, giving a little twist to seat it firmly. Cut the tab to the appropriate length with a blade or scissors. When the button is dry, file or scrape the edges of the tab to make a neat, rounded edge.

Fire upside-down on a bed of alumina hydrate or vermiculite.

Small Spoon

Small spoons like this can be used for sugar, relish and condiments. Perhaps more important than the function is the way these family heirlooms celebrate the special occasions of life. Because fine silver is a soft metal, spoons should not be much larger than three inches.

Pull off a grape-sized piece of paper clay and roll it into a sphere. Cut the sphere in half and allow it to dry.

Roll a sheet of PMC to the thickness of a dime (4 cards, 1.4 mm) and cut from it a circle about 3/4" (18 mm) in diameter. Press the circle over the paper clay to make the bowl of the spoon, then set it aside to dry.

Roll out a tapered rod of PMC about 4" long and at least 3/16" thick at the larger end. Slightly flatten the larger end of the taper by pressing it with your fingers or rolling it with a plastic pipe. Slice this end into two arms and roll these between your fingers to make them round.

Open the arms of the rod and set the dome into the notch, forming the two strands into graceful curves that reach up around the bowl of the spoon. Moisten the joint and press the pieces together to seal them. Add PMC slurry to reinforce the joint.

Bend the other end into a graceful loop and wrap the taper around the shaft of the spoon. You might consider placing a gemstone here.

Fire right-side up on a bed of alumina hydrate or vermiculite.
Burnish or tumble as usual.

Sugar Scoop

This unusual sugar scoop is just one of dozens of serving pieces you can make to bring special personality to your entertaining occasions. Other possibilities include pickle forks, salt dishes, candle holders and snuffers. This piece shows how you can combine PMC with non-metal pieces. Here I've used a twig; other possibilities include polymer clay, carved wood, ceramic or glass.

Make a paper pattern of the finished size of the bowl section. Cut the desired form from stiff paper and score the lines by going over them with a pen so they will fold neatly. Use tiny bits of tape to hold the form closed temporarily. When the size seems correct, open the pattern and photocopy it to adjust for shrinkage. For original PMC, set the machine to 135%. For PMC+ or PMC3, use 115%. Cut out the enlargement and trace it to create the bowl scoop element.

Roll out a sheet of PMC about the thickness of a dime (4 cards, 1.4 mm) and cut around the pattern with a blade or a card. To crease the fold lines, press a ruler or a credit card halfway through the sheet. To create a texture, I've pressed a leaf into the sheet.

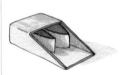

Pull the sides up and press the corners together to seal them. Smooth the joints by rubbing with a fingernail or blunt tool. Set the piece aside to dry. If the clay is very soft and starts to sag, temporarily set a folded piece of paper into the scoop.

Make a ferrule to attach the handle to the scoop. Wrap the twig with several layers of tape — this will "enlarge" the handle to compensate for shrinkage in firing. Roll a rectangular strip of PMC around this to make a tube. The ferrule can be ornamented or plain and can have molding applied like this one or not. Seal the joint on the ferrule and blend until the joint disappears.

Dampen the bottom rim of the ferrule (or apply a layer of slip) and press it firmly onto the back wall of the scoop. This is a critical joint so it should be reinforced for strength. Set the assembly aside to dry, propping as needed to keep the parts in the correct angle.

The cap for the end of the handle is a lot like the ferrule. Make a cylinder and set it, opening up, onto a sheet of PMC. Cut away extra and seal the joint. You might find it helpful to set the cap loosely onto the end of a pen or pencil as you work.

To ornament the cap with a gem (optional), I'll add a ball of PMC large enough to surround the stone. Press it into place and flatten into a thick stump. With a pencil point, poke a conical hole in the center of the lump, rotating the pencil to enlarge the angle. Press the gem into the hole until it is just below the surface. For more information on embedding gemstones see page 92.

Fire the pieces as usual and finish in a way that best shows off the surface. In this example I've chosen to leave the piece matte (as opposed to burnishing it) and have darkened it with commercial patina. See page 99 for details.

Use epoxy to attach the pieces, taking care to wipe away all excess. If you have metalworking experience, you might want to drill through the handle and add a rivet.

Beverage Sticks

Have you ever had a drink that wears its own jewelry? Imagine a silver swizzle stick in a fancy drink, or a silver pick to skewer a martini olive. How about a silver straw with the family crest or a personalized coffee stirrer for that very special reception? From weddings to anniversaries to corporate functions, you'll think of lots of ways to expand this idea to fit your needs. This example uses a candy mold to make a spoon bowl, but bear in mind that you could make this in other ways or omit that part altogether.

The shaft of the stirrer will be a tube of anodized aluminum, making this piece a straw as well as a stirrer. Other options include a solid aluminum rod (use a knitting needle) or a sterling tube. Whatever you use, it will be necessary to create a surface to connect the PMC pieces to the stem.

To make a cradle to attach the pieces to the tube, start by cutting two rectangles of PMC and draping them over a rod (pen, drinking straw, etc.) to mold them into a curve. Dampen the center of this piece and press the ornament firmly into it. Set the pieces aside to dry, propped up as necessary.

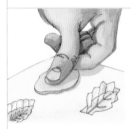

Candy molds are great for PMC; they're inexpensive, easily available and come in a wide variety of shapes. Visit a hobby or kitchen supply store or check out the mail order suppliers listed at the end of this book. The clear plastic panels that have about a dozen molds are the cheapest and work as well for PMC as the more expensive rubber or ceramic styles. It's okay to lubricate the mold with a little olive oil or cooking spray, but that is not usually necessary.

Pull off a lump of PMC and roll it into a ball. Press it into a flat patty and set this into the mold. With a fingertip or blunt tool squeeze the clay into the mold, thinning it evenly as you press it into every corner. Gently lift and edge and coax the PMC out of the mold.

Dampen the joint and press the bowl of the spoon against one of the cradle pieces. Reinforce the joint with slip.

To make the ornament, roll out a sheet of PMC (4 cards, 1.4 mm) and cut out a monogram, a playful shape or a numeral (for a birthday or anniversary). You can make a matched set of beverage sticks or make each one unique.

Fire and finish as usual.

Glue the pieces onto tubing or rod with epoxy.

Thimble

How many people do you know who have a handmade pure silver thimble? Here's a perfect gift that is both practical and collectable. This example uses stars, but you'll see that the decorative technique shown below has many other uses.

Make a form from Styrofoam, wood, plaster or papier maché to work on. This should be a little bigger than a standard thimble to allow for shrinkage. Make the form of a material that will burn away, or plan on pulling the thimble off before firing. Wrap paper around the form and draw on it to create a pattern for the cone and the top, which you can cut from the paper with scissors. You'll end up with a wide arch shape and a circle.

Roll out a slab of PMC about as thick as a dime (4 cards, 1.4 mm) and trace the paper patterns to make the two pieces that will form the thimble.

Wrap the PMC arc around the form, thinning and overlapping the ends slightly. Set the circle cap into place and smooth all joints with a blunt tool or your fingernail.

Roll out a thin slab and cut out a star to fit on top. Moisten both surfaces and press them together. Of course you can use any other shape or skip this step altogether.

Make the band for the bottom edge by slicing a strip from a thick narrow slab. Moisten the bottom of the thimble and press the band into position. Handle the joint as you did the body of the thimble, squeezing to thin each end, overlapping and rubbing until the seam disappears.

Texture the thimble — I used the tip of a knitting needle to make a pattern of dimples. These have the functional advantage of catching the end of a needle when the thimble is used, but some thimbles are left smooth.

Dry, fire and finish as recommended.

Picture Frame

Here's a wonderful idea for that person who has everything. This example is orna-mented with Syringe Style PMC but other designs can be made by texturing and lay-ering standard PMC. This example is designed to sit on a desk or table, but a frame could be modified to be worn as a brooch.

2

Roll out a sheet of PMC at least as thick as a dime (4 cards, 1.4 mm). Mark out the center hole and determine the overall shape of the frame.

Cut the internal hole for the photo.

Roll out additional PMC and cut narrow stips to create a lattice structure on the front of the frame. Lay these pieces into position, add a drop of water and press them lightly to secure them to the sheet.

A special consistency of PMC is sold loaded into a plastic syringe. Alternately, you can make the syringe described on page 116. Squeeze out a thread of PMC to draw an ornamental pattern around the frame. If the thread breaks, overlap the lines and continue.

Cut away PMC to make the outer edges of the desired shape.

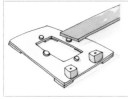

Allow the frame to dry for at least 15 minutes so it can be moved without damaging the detail. Flip the piece over and add a ball of fresh PMC in the center of each edge. These will be used to hold the photo in place.

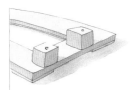

To make a stand for the frame we'll add two thick sections on the back. Roll out a thick slab of PMC and cut two blocks about 1/4" (6 mm) on each side. Press these onto the back near the bottom edge. Poke a hole in each with a needle tool.

Fire flat at the recommended temperature. Finish with steel wool, a nylon pad or pumice, or by tumbling. Patina with a darkening agent or leave the silver bright.

Cut a piece of wire (sterling, paper clip, etc.) and bend a U-shaped loop that will lock into the holes in the blocks.

To secure a picture (photo, drawing, tintype), loop a small dental rubber band or a piece of thread around the balls on the back of the frame.

Tea Strainer

Here's an advanced project for ambitious PMC users. This silver tea infuser is guaranteed to add elegance to any brew. Fine silver will not be harmed by tea and in fact has the ability to kill germs!

Roll out a sheet of PMC that will become the outer rim. In addition to its decorative aspect, this is what holds the tea strainer above the cup. On stiff paper, draw a hexagonal pattern with a compass and ruler, then cut out the shape to make a template. Cut out the hexagon and the inside circle (which is the same size as the dome).

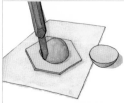

Find or make a half sphere on which to build a form. This could be molded from papier maché or made by cutting a ball in half. Set this onto the PMC sheet that will become the rim of the infuser and seal it into place with slip.

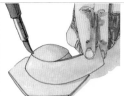

Cover the dome with a layer of PMC at least 4 cards thick (1.4 mm). Use various pieces to cover the form, sealing the joints with a dampened finger.

Cut strips of PMC and add them to the outer edges of the hexagon to thicken and reinforce the lip.

Allow the piece to dry and remove the dome form by gently pulling it out. Harden the strainer by baking it in a kitchen oven for about 15 minutes at 300°-350° F. File or sand the edges and surfaces to make neat joints and straight lines.

If you wish, add carved lines to the top hexagonal plate.

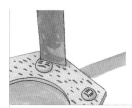

In this piece, I have added hexagrams from the I-Ching, an ancient Chinese system of symbols. You could use any other ornament or skip this altogether. The symbols used here were chosen to relate to the reflective nature of tea: contemplation, keeping still, society, understanding, nourishment and pleasure.

To support the piece for firing, nestle it deeply into a ceramic container filled with vermiculite or alumina hydrate. Fire as recommended.

The hexagonal plate will probably warp a little during firing. To flatten it, set the piece upside down on a table top and tap it lightly with a mallet or use pliers as shown to smooth out minor irregularities.

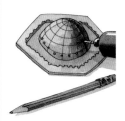

To make this function as a tea infuser you will need to drill many holes. These can be randomly placed, but in this case I decided to locate them symmetrically around the bottom. Draw guidelines with a pencil, then drill the holes with a small bit. Sand the silver to remove small burs. PMC does not require a special drill bit; a conventional bit from the hardware store will work.

Box with Textured Surface

This is a challenging project that shows a use for PMC paste. Though not essential to the project, the construction method shown here uses conventional sterling silver sheet to make the bottom of the box. This alternative construction method conserves on material while providing greater control.

This box was made on a cardboard tube from wrapping paper. Of course you can make your own form from cardboard. Start by coating it in masking tape so it won't suck moisture out of the PMC as you work. I've cut off a piece about 8" long to make it more convenient to hold.

Roll out a sheet of PMC 5 cards thick (3 mm, 3/32") and long enough to go around the tube. This box is one inch tall. Wrap the sheet around the tube so that about 1/8" (3 mm) hangs off one end. Close and seal the joint.

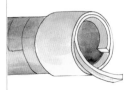

Roll out another strip of PMC, this one a little thicker and a lot narrower. This will make a ledge that will hold the bottom which will be laid into place after the wall of the box has been fired. Dampen the part that overhangs the tube and lay the strip into the overhanging area, pressing it firmly onto the wall as you go around. Cut to length and seal the seam.

PMC paste can be purchased ready to use or made by mixing standard PMC with water. Spread a layer of paste onto the box using those skills you've been practicing on your toast each morning. Use a standard knife, a plastic knife, a palette knife or even your finger.

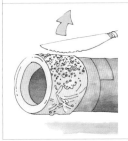

When you have an even layer, go back over the paste, pressing the tool down then lifting it abruptly away. This is one way to make an interesting texture and you can experiment to find other textures you like.

Cut off the excess cardboard tube with scissors. If the tube inside the PMC box pulls away easily, remove it, but don't risk accidentally damaging the box by tugging at it too hard. It will burn out harmlessly in the first stage of firing.

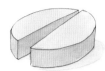

Make a handle of PMC by cutting a disk from a thick sheet and cutting it in half. Use one part and return the other to your PMC supply. Coat the half disk with paste to create the same texture as on the box.

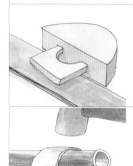

Attach a flat strip that will hold the handle onto the lid. Roll out a sheet and cut a hole, then cut a part of this and attach it to the bottom edge of the half disk handle.

Fire the box in the usual way.

Don't be surprised if your box gets distorted during firing. In fact, be surprised if it doesn't. The advantage of making the box without a bottom is that the distortion is quite easy to correct. Set the box over any convenient cylinder — a jar, a bottle, a pipe, etc. — and tap the form back into round with a mallet or a piece of wood.

Carefully measure the diameter in several places across the form and use an average to determine the size of a disk that will become the bottom. This can be silver, copper, brass, wood, polymer clay or plastic depending on your skills and the effect you want to create. Cut this disk a little oversize, then file or sand it until it can be pressed down against the bottom rim. The idea is to make this such a tight fit that friction alone will hold the bottom in the box. It might be necessary to lightly tap the metal into position with a short piece of wood.

To make a wooden lid like the one shown here, cut a disk that just fits inside the box and another that is a little larger. File and sand to a pleasing shape. Of course, this piece could also be made of polymer clay, ceramic, etc. Glue the two pieces together.

Cut a slot for the handle element and insert its tab. Slide a wedge through the hole to lock it in place.

Miniature Teapot

There is a special pleasure in making familiar objects in a miniature size. This silver teapot would grace any dollhouse, and once you finish this you can move on to make trays, silver serving pieces, candlesticks and other housewares.

Use a pen, a dowel or a rod made of paper maché or paper clay to make a core that will be the internal volume of the pot.

Roll out a thick rod of PMC and cut it in half along its length to make a half-round rod. Roll this around the core, then moisten and burnish the seams to create a rounded body for the pot. Add a disk to cap off the bottom (the pot is upside down on the rod at this point).

Pull the form off the core and thicken the rim of the pot by adding a thin wire of PMC. When the shape is correct, allow the piece to dry and/or heat it slowly in a kitchen oven to drive off the moisture. Refine the form with sandpaper.

Roll out a taper of PMC and cut the end at an angle so it will blend neatly onto the pot. Dampen the area of attachment and dab some PMC slurry there. If you are copying a piece that has a wooden handle, either make the whole piece in PMC and paint the "wooden" part or make sockets in the PMC and add a handle of polymer clay.

Make a lid by cutting a sphere of PMC in half. Add a disk that will fit inside the rim of the pot and trim with a knife or sandpaper to make a snug fit. Press a hole into the top of the lid and press a small piece of PMC into place to make a finial.

Fire as recommended, keeping the pot and lid separate. Finish with a scratchbrush and sand if necessary to make the pot sit flat and to allow the lid to drop into place.

Part Two
TECHNICAL TIPS

Designing for PMC

PMC is a wonderful and durable material, but, like any other substance it has its limitations. Experience and observation will guide you as you discover what PMC does best. To start the process, here are some facts:

- PMC is made of pure silver, technically called fine silver. This metal is about 20-30% softer than sterling, which is in turn almost twice as malleable as 14K yellow gold.
- Fine silver is second only to pure gold in malleability and ductility. Of all metals, silver is the best conductor of electricity and heat.
- Fine silver does not tarnish, which is why it is used in fillings and electrical contacts. Because it is so soft (a.k.a "gummy") it is resistant to abrasion and slightly more difficult to drill than sterling or brass.

This means is that PMC is ideally suited to substantial objects that will be either polished or given a matte finish. It is not recommended for thin wires or objects that will be under stress. Here are a few examples to illustrate what to avoid when designing pieces that will be made in Precious Metal Clay. These guidelines are intended to alert you to specific concerns and should be interpreted by each individual artist.

Fine silver is not a particularly strong metal, either when milled as conventional sheet and wire or as PMC. Avoid creating thin fingers that are likely to get snagged and bent. Instead, connect small extensions to make a continous structure. Think like a spider.

To avoid stresses on a relatively fragile material, use moving parts whenever possible. In the case of this bail, for instance, the example on the right is far more likely to withstand rough treatment. The sterling ring will also hold up better to the friction caused by the rubbing of the chain in the loop.

In a large scale as well as small, use joints to protect stress areas against fatigue. The bracelet on the left would need to be quite thick to stand up to use, but the jointed bracelet on the right will yield to bumps and can therefore use less metal to achieve the same practicality.

Working Surfaces

Where do you work with PMC? The kitchen table? A professional studio? In the den? About all you need is a flat surface and good lighting, so people are probably using PMC in all sorts of places. As far as the actual working surface, all you need is a non-porous material in a convenient size. You can work directly on the tabletop or kitchen counter, but working on a notebook-size panel makes it easier to rotate, angle and move the piece. Here are a few ideas.

Glass

You might find scraps or ready-cut pieces in a handy size. Either ask the vendor to grind the edges smooth or cover them with a strong tape to prevent risk of cuts.

Advantages: smooth, can't be cut
Disadvantages: breakable, heavy

Plexiglas

Again, you might find useful scraps by calling a glass company or checking with a local window company. Sheets of Plexi are usually available at hardware stores and lumber yards.

Advantages: won't break, lightweight, cheap
Disadvantages: knife cuts will leave marks

Light Panel

Light panels for drop ceilings can be bought at lumber yards and some hardware stores. These panels have a texture on one side that not only makes an interesting texture for PMC work, but a handy drying rack. Set a piece on the textured side to allow air to circulate around it. To cut the large panel, score a line with a knife and snap.

Advantages: lightweight, cheap
Disadvantages: brittle, sometimes wavy, retains knifemarks if you cut on it

PVC Board

Art supply stores sell a plastic mat board that makes a great work surface for PMC. This 1/8" plastic panel can be broken into convenient pieces by scoring a line with a ruler and a knife. A sharp bending action usually yields a clean line. If you don't care about the color, ask for scrap pieces.

Advantages: light, durable, colorful
Disadvantages: knife cuts will leave marks

Non-stick Baking Sheets

These paper-thin Teflon films are sold in kitchen supply stores. It seems like nothing sticks to them, so they offer a wonderful surface for PMC.

Advantages: durable, non-stick
Disadvantages: cost

Placemats and Plastic Signs

Occaisionly I run across sheets of plastic that were intended for some other use but also make great work surfaces for PMC. At full price these are not cost effective, but when I see them on sale I pick up a handful.

Advantages: easy to cut, cheap, disposable
Disadvantages: thin, pattern can be distracting

Countertop Laminate

Contact local cabinetmakers or architectural woodworkers about scraps of Formica or similar products.

Advantages: tough, resilient
Disadvantages: doesn't break well, cost

Rehydrating PMC

Precious Metal Clay is at its optimum consistency when it is shipped from the factory. It will hold this consistency for as long as a year if the package is not opened, but eventually it can dry out. The good news is that it can be re-moistened. Experience and feel are your best teachers in this, but here are some suggestions, listed from least dry to most dry.

Fresh

Approximately 10% water. When squeezed between a forefinger and thumb, a lump will press out into a smooth patty and show fingerprints clearly.

This is the ideal consistency. PMC is double wrapped at the factory and stored in humidors to insure that each package is fresh. A use-by date is stamped on each box to remind users which units should be opened first. Leave packages sealed until you are ready to use the PMC and reseal unused portions immediately by rewrapping in plastic film.

Firm

Approximately 5-8% water. Squeezing a lump requires effort; edges start to show small cracks.

To make this sample softer, poke the lump repeatedly with a needle to make dozens of holes. Spritz or brush with water and allow the piece to sit for several minutes. Knead the plastic-wrapped PMC to force the water throughout the sample. If possible, allow the PMC to sit for an hour or more before use. If you can't wait, expect the material to be a little stickier than usual.

Apple Hard

Approximately 3-5% water. Cannot be flattened by squeezing in the fingers, but there is a bit of flexibility; rubbery.

Dice the PMC as you would cut up garlic in the kitchen. Use a sharp blade (paring knife, X-Acto, tissue blade) and chop the PMC into tiny pieces, ideally no larger than 1/16" (1.6 mm).

Collect these in a plastic container and add just enough water to cover the pieces. Allow to soak for at least an hour — overnight is OK. Stir the resulting PMM (precious metal mud) with a knife, palette knife or your finger, pressing out any lumps that may remain. If the dicing was appropriately fine there will be very few lumps. If the mud is lumpy, make a mental note to dice into finer pieces next time. Add just enough water to wet the surface and again allow the mix to sit for at least an hour. Roll the mud onto a sheet of plastic film, wrap it up and knead the lump thoroughly to work out any remaining lumps.

Rock Hard

Approximately 0-3% water. Makes a knocking sound when tapped on a table.

Cut the PMC into small pieces and grind them in a pepper mill, catching the particles on a sheet of paper. To further reduce the size of the pieces, run the grain through the mill two or three times. Repeat as needed. Allow two days to rehydrate a PMR (precious metal rock).

Using Slip

Because PMC is water soluble, it can be thinned with water to make a paste called slip or slurry. To make slip, set a bit of fresh PMC on a flat plastic or glass surface and add a small quantity of water. With a plastic blade (e.g. picnic knife, ruler or pallette knife) smear the PMC and water together, pressing in several directions alternately. The goal is to make a material with the consistency of toothpaste. Add water or more PMC as needed.

To make slip from dry PMC, start by cutting or grinding the clay into small pieces. Dice with a sharp knife or grind in a pepper mill to make pieces no larger than one millimeter in any direction. Put these in a small container, add enough water to cover the pieces and set aside for at least an hour so the moisture can soak in. Transfer the resulting PMM (precious metal mud) to a flat plastic or glass surface and smear the PMC to squeeze out lumps and make a homogenous creamy slip.

To make slip from fresh PMC, pull off a small piece, perhaps the size of a pea, and place it on a flat sheet of glass or plastic. Add several drops of water and smear the two together with a flexible knife. A plastic pallette knife, a picnic knife or a strip of plastic all work well.

Once you have some slip started it's easy to keep up a supply. At the end of each working session, pick up the tiny bits and pieces that are (inevitably) sprinkled on the table and drop them into your slip jar. This can be any container — a small jar, a kitchen container, or a film canister all work well. Add a few drops of water and seal the jar. When you need slip, just stir the mix and you'll find it ready to use.

Slip can be used as a glue to cement pieces together. It is especially good for irregular surfaces.

Slip makes an interesting surface all by itself. Spread it on with a knife, like frosting on a cake.

Use slip to fill small splits that sometimes appear as a piece dries.

Brush or spread slip in a joint to create a fillet, the rounded contour that strengthens a seam.

Extruding

As it is manufactured, all versions of PMC are too thick to be squeezed through a nozzle. To extrude it, the material will require modification in one of three ways:

1. Thin the PMC with water.
2. Increase leverage.
3. Use reformulated material.

1. As described on the preceding page, PMC can be mixed with water to create a thin material called slip. This can be loaded into a syringe or similar tool and squeezed out easily. Plastic syringes are sold at hardware stores for use with epoxies. Pastry tubes, children's toys, kitchen devices and scientific equipment offer other possibilities.

   The drawback of this system is that the extruded bead (or trail) will lose definition before it dries. What at first appears to be a rounded thread will sag into a flat mass within a few minutes. As a way to supply slip to a work or create texture, extruded slip can be useful, but it does not lend itself to building up forms.

2. To push standard PMC through an extruder, normal hand pressure needs to be increased. One way to accomplish this is with a threaded mechanism like the make-it-yourself extruder shown on page 116. Another variation is to use a caulking gun in conjunction with an extruder like the Klay gun sold through ceramic suppliers.

3. The manufacturer of PMC has reformulated the basic material to create a substance that is thin enough to extrude but able to resist sagging. This version is available in PMC+ and fires at the same temperatures as the lump and paste versions. Standard and extruded material can be mixed in a single piece.

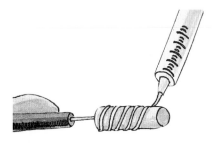 

Carving PMC

The first thing anyone notices about Precious Metal Clay is how soft it is. The putty-like consistency makes it possible to mold PMC easily. Sometimes, though, the plastic quality of PMC can be too much of a good thing. There are times when a design calls for a crisp edge or precise line that is easier to achieve when the object is semi-dry, a condition potters call leather hard.

To conserve material and save time, the piece is given its general shape while the PMC is soft. Roll out sheets, build up layers, wrap a core and so on to create the desired form. Allow the work to dry naturally by setting it aside unwrapped. Depending on the thickness of the piece and the ambient humidity, this could take anywhere from one hour (on a summer windowsill) to overnight (in a spring fog).

Pieces will dry more uniformly if air is allowed to circulate across all sides. Set the work on plastic mesh (rug hooking) or a crumpled up paper. Most of the water in PMC will evaporate naturally, leaving a material with the consistency of soap. This makes it easy to carve.

Forced Drying

To speed up the drying process, set the work in a kitchen oven and heat to 250° F for about 15 minutes. This will drive off the moisture. **TIP**: Use this bake-to-harden trick if you want to protect your work from breaking. It's especially useful if you are mailing an unfired piece or if there will be a long delay before firing. The delay doesn't affect the PMC in any way but a wait extends the time when a piece can be damaged by accidental rough handling.

Carving Tools

Wood carving and linoleum tools work well on semi-hard PMC. They can be purchased at art supply and hobby craft shops. People with some metalworking experience will be able to make their own tools from bicycle spokes, dental tools, steel rods, coat hangers, welding rods and nails. File whatever shapes will be most useful and hone them with fine grit sandpaper. Handles can be made from wood or polymer clay or by wrapping the shaft of a tool with cord to improve the grip.

Shavings

The small curls of PMC that result from the carving process can be re-moistened (see page 80) or used as a texture. To collect the shavings, work over a piece of stiff paper.

Making Holes

The best time to make holes in PMC is while it is soft. Not only is it easiest, but this way the material that is removed can be reused most efficiently.

Plastic Straws

Plastic straws and beverage stirrers make great hole-cutting tools. They are cheap and easy to find. To use them, simply press straight down and rotate the straw. Usually the PMC being removed sticks into the straw. To remove it, blow on the other end and catch the PMC as it shoots out. Sometimes you'll need to pinch the straw to extract the plug.

If you use a lot of holes, you may want to make a device that will simplify the removal process. First you'll need to find a rod that fits into the straw you are using. A wooden dowel, plastic rod, pencil or knitting needle will work. Cut and file the ends so they are flat and smooth. To push and pull the plunger, make a ring from wire that will fit on your index finger. Nothing fancy here — a straightened paper clip will work. Poke the wire into the plunger and secure it with glue. To use, just press the straw through the PMC with the plunger raised, extract the plug, then press the plunger to pop it out. In addition to making holes, this is an easy way to make a lot of identical disks.

Larger Holes

Cookie cutters are sold by kitchenware and ceramic supply companies in round sizes from about a half inch up to three inches. A set of concentric biscuit cutters is very useful. To make your own metal cutters see page 114.

After Firing

Sometimes it's better to wait until after the firing to make holes. The edge created with a drill bit will be neater and the shape will be more precise. You can use any drill bit on silver, either by hand or with an electric drill. Avoid fast speeds and lubricate the bit with beeswax or paraffin.

If a drill bit isn't cutting, it has probably become dull. Pushing harder on the drill won't help! Drill bits can be sharpened, but usually the best solution is to use a new bit. To enlarge a hole, use a tapered round file or a tapered reamer.

Smoothing Edges

Here are a few suggestions for handling edges. These techniques can be used separately or in any combination when a smooth polished edge is desired. Of course in some designs the naturally dried and cracked PMC might best complement the design.

When the PMC is soft

Cut with a sharp knife to make a crisp smooth edge.

     ... or ...

Moisten your fingertip and rub it lightly along an edge to reshape it and smooth it at the same time.

     ... or ...

Use a damp brush over an edge to round it and remove tool marks or fingerprints.

When the PMC is dried but not fired

Use sandpaper or an emery board to smooth and refine the edges.

     ... or ...

Scrape an edge with a knife blade held at right angles to the edge. A utility knife, paring knife or even a piece of glass will work well.

     ... or ...

Burnish an edge by rubbing it firmly with a polished steel tool — a stainless steel spoon, nut pick or large nail will work.

After firing

All of the sanding and burnishing techniques listed above can be used after firing. In addition, you can use files and mechanical grinders. In hardware stores you can buy "flap wheels" — pieces of sandpaper attached to a hub that is clamped into an electric drill.

Ring Sizing

Getting the size correct is especially important when it comes to rings. Too small and we can't get them on. Too large and we are afraid our rings will drop off and get lost. Ring sizing is always a challenge for jewelers because people's hands change size, not only over the years, but in some cases, from hour to hour. And to make matters even more confusing, numerical ring sizes refer to several competing systems and are famously inexact.

The following information is intended to lead most people to a successful size, most of the time. These dimensions assume a ring of average thickness (1.5 mm for small sizes, 2 mm for larger) and a width of about 6 mm, or 1/4". If your ring is very wide, make it a half size larger than normal. Start by wrapping a piece of paper around the knuckle of the finger for which you are making the ring. When making for someone else, try one of their rings (or the ring sizer) onto your hand to find one of your fingers that matches.

Ring Size	Metal	PMC+ PMC 3	PMC
2	44.6 mm	50.7 mm	61.9 mm
2 1/2	45.8	52.0	63.6
3	47.1	53.5	65.4
3 1/2	48.4	55.0	67.2
4	49.6	56.4	68.8
4 1/2	50.9	57.8	70.7
5	52.1	59.2	72.4
5 1/2	53.4	60.7	74.2
6	54.6	62.0	75.8
6 1/2	55.9	63.5	77.6
7	57.1	64.8	79.3
7 1/2	58.4	66.4	81.1
8	59.7	67.8	82.9
8 1/2	60.9	69.2	84.6
9	62.2	70.7	86.4
9 1/2	63.4	72.0	88.0
10	64.7	73.5	89.9
10 1/2	65.9	74.8	91.5
11	67.2	76.4	93.3
11 1/2	68.5	77.8	95.1
12	69.7	79.2	96.8
12 1/2	71.0	80.7	98.6
13	72.2	82.0	100.3

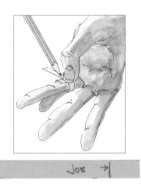

JOE →

Rigid Molds

When you enter the world of molds, you dramatically increase your options. Molds make it possible to work faster and with greater consistency than shaping each piece one at a time. Molds are used in several of the projects in this book.

Press molds are the simplest and most useful for PMC. These are reverse images of an intended form, made in any material harder than the stuff being formed. To use them, the clay is simply pressed into the mold then lifted out. Because PMC is so pliable, press molds can be made of wood, plastics, papier-maché, ceramic and metal. The following categories describe a few of the options that await your investigation.

Polymer Clay

Fimo, Primo, Sculpey, etc. can all be used for mold making. Because color is irrelevant to this use, molds are a great way to make use of odd mixtures and miscellaneous scraps. To capture an existing pattern or shape, press softened polymer over the form. You can also build a mold by layering, texturing and modeling the polymer. Remember that the PMC object will be about 25-30% smaller and the reverse of the mold. A cavity in the mold will be a raised element in the final piece. Harden the polymer following manufacturers instructions.

Undercuts

Press molds are pretty simple but there is one important trick. What gets pressed in has to get pulled out. If the mold wall is vertical, pulling will probably be OK. If the wall slopes inward slightly (called drift) the piece will pop out even better. If the cavity gets wider as it gets deeper, or if there is a lip, we would describe the mold as having an undercut. PMC can be pressed in easily enough, but it cannot be removed without damaging the form.

AVOID undercuts. If the form you're making absolutely requires them, the first recourse is to use a flexible mold material, described on the next page. This will accommodate some minor undercuts. In extreme cases it might be necessary to make a two-part mold or to cut the object into parts that can be molded separately.

Plastic

Thermosetting plastic materials are available through art supply or medical supply companies (they are used to make splints). Brand names include Protoplast, JettSett and Friendly Plastic. The material is available in the form of sheets, rods, mesh and pellets.

1. Get a cup of hot water, either from the tap or by making boiling water in a tea kettle or microwave. Drop in some of the pellets and watch them change from opaque to translucent.
2. After about a minute, fish out the glob of the now-soft plastic and squeeze it together to force out air pockets. The plastic will have the consistency of chewing gum.
3. Press it onto a texture or over a form, pushing down firmly to eliminate air bubbles.
4. Either allow the mold to cool naturally, or hold it under cold water. When it is hard to the touch (usually a couple of minutes), pull the plastic from the model.
5. Thermosetting plastics are reusable. At any time in the future you can simply drop this mold into hot water and start over.

Flexible Molds

Vulcanized Molds

The jewelry industry relies heavily on molds that are made by curing raw rubber under heat and pressure to make a durable rubber mold. Many craft schools and colleges have the tools necessary for this process and there are dozens of casting companies around the country who will make these molds from your original. They are usually designed as a two-part mold into which molten wax can be injected to make multiples for the lost wax casting process. PMC requires only an open mold.

Chemically Set Rubber Molds

Recent developments in the technology of mold-making have created a wide variety of options in mold materials. Among the best for work on a jewelry scale are two-part compounds that trigger a chemical reaction when they are combined. There are dozens of variations on this technology, which is sometimes known as Room Temperature Vulcanizing (RTV) or Cold Mold Compound (CMC).

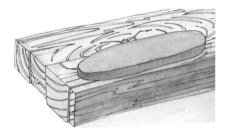

   This putty-like material has the double advantage of easy handling and fast curing. Three popular brands are Belicold, Mega-Sil and Exaflex (see appendix for sources). Price and setting time vary slightly but the instructions for use are the same.

Making a Flexible Mold from a Two-Part Compound

1. Pull equal quantities from the two containers. Roll the separate pieces into a ball or rod to make it easier to compare sizes.
2. Knead the lumps together until the "fudge swirl" effect disappears and the mass has a uniform color.
3. Press the putty onto an object (or an object into the putty) and set it aside.
4. After 10-20 minutes, poke the mold with your fingernail — if it leaves an impression, the mold has not cured yet. If the mold feels springy, pull it off the model.

Caulking as a Mold

An industrious (or desperate) PMC user might sometimes need to make a mold in a hurry from locally available resources. One possibility is bathtub caulking, a silicone-based air hardening rubber that is sold in most hardware stores. Follow the directions on the tube, particularly the part about kneading the material to soften it. The soft paste will harden into a pliable rubber, usually in a few hours, though some brands take overnight to cure.

These are excellent adhesives, which means they will hold onto the model very well. If you're taking an impression of something that you don't mind losing (like a piece of wood, for instance) you can probably pick it out of the mold in pieces. For a harder substance like a seashell, metal button, etc., coat the model with a layer of olive oil before spreading on the caulk.

Alginate

This is a soft mold material familiar to anyone who had braces as a child. Alginate has been a standard mold material in dentistry for years. It is sold through medical and jewelry supply companies as a soft powder that is mixed with water. The advantage of alginate is that it sets up within a few minutes and takes a detailed impression. The disadvantage is that the mold will only last for a day before it starts to dry out, becoming misshapen and rigid.

Using Molds

In most cases the process requires no lubrication or special tools. Push some PMC into the mold using a rolling pin to create an even pressure. Pull it out, either by tugging gingerly at the edges or by inverting the mold and flexing it to release the PMC object.

If the PMC sticks and the form is distorted in trying to remove it, scrape out the PMC and roll it into a ball. Put a couple drops of olive oil on your hands and roll the ball between your palms. This will create a thin film of lubricating oil on the surface of the PMC. If that technique fails after several tries, remove the PMC and spray the mold lightly with a cooking spray. If none of these methods works there might be a problem with the mold.

To make a hollow-backed object, press your finger or a tool into the lump of PMC as it is going into the mold. To expand on this idea, make a second mold for the back, either by carving it from a strong material like wood, plastic or plaster, or by molding it from polymer clay. To do this, first create the desired shape in your original. If this is PMC, allow the piece to dry, then bake it for a few minutes in an oven to further harden it.

Press properly conditioned polymer clay into the socket and mold the top part to make a comfortable tool. Withdraw carefully and cure the polymer according to the manufacturer's instructions. Press a bit of PMC into the mold, then complete the molding process by pressing it further with the plug.

Shrinkage

Precious Metal Clay shrinks when it is fired. In some cases, that's all you need to know — make it big and enjoy the dazzling detail when it's done. In some cases, though, it is useful to have a better understanding of how and why the shrinkage occurs. Standard PMC shrinks by about 28%. PMC+ and PMC3 shrink by about 12%. The discrepancy is the result of differing amounts of metal, binder and water, but the concept is the same for both materials.

Precious Metal Clay consists of tiny particles of metal cloaked in a film of moist binder. This is what gives the material its clay-like consistency and allows it to be worked easily in the fingers. Picture PMC particles as chocolate covered peanuts. A given quantity of them will take up a specific volume of space. Now imagine taking off the chocolate and putting the peanuts back into a cluster. It will be smaller, right? The difference between the space occupied by coated and uncoated peanuts would depend on the thickness of the chocolate. In Standard PMC, the coating represents about 28% of the total volume. In PMC+ and PMC3, it constitutes about 12%.

But we're not quite done. Imagine breaking the nuts into small pieces and again measuring the volume being taken up. Because the spaces between the particles are smaller, the same mass takes up less room. This is analogous to what happens when PMC is heated in a kiln, a process called sintering.

The water in the PMC burns off at around 100° C (212° F) depending on your location above sea level. The binder catches fire and burns up soon after. If you were to open the kiln at exactly the right moment, you will see your work enveloped in flame. This lasts for less than a minute and creates a fleeting odor similar to an oven spill in the kitchen. Because most of the change in PMC comes from the removal of the water and binder, most of the shrinkage will occur during this stage of the process. After about a half hour in a kiln, the pieces have shed the binder and water and have pretty much reached their final size.

At this point there is almost nothing holding the metal particles together. This allows shapes to slump as gravity pulls them down. If work was removed from the kiln at this point, you'd find that it looks like metal but feels lightweight. It would take a shine when burnished but could never get to a bright mirror polish. Most alarming, you'd find that you could snap the piece in two with your fingers.

As the temperature in the kiln approaches the melting point of the metal, the outer surface of each particle becomes fluid and flows into the adjacent particles. This further reduces the size of the object, but because the spaces being closed are so tiny, the percentage of shrinkage at this point is very slight. This is the point at which the particles fuse into a solid mass, making the metal hard.

How to Guide Shrinkage

It's possible, after some experience, to steer the shrinkage by making cuts in strategic places. Think of the way gussets are cut into a coat around the arms and back to allow the garment to expand without ripping. They accommodate the stress by anticipating it. In a similar way, you can make cuts with a sharp knife to provide a place for the PMC to give. These will grow into V-shaped openings during sintering and can be worked into the design of a piece.

Standard PMC Ruler

Use the ruler shown here to gauge shrinkage of standard PMC (roughly 28%). Photocopy, fold and glue the ruler to make it double sided. To make them more durable, these rulers can be laminated in clear plastic.

One side of the ruler allows you to predict the size of the work after firing. Suppose you have a cookie cutter and want to know how big a piece made from it will be after firing. Measure the tool (or a piece cut with it) with the actual ruler (marked with the word "inches") then find this number on the reduced scale marked **After Firing**. This will be the approximate size of the piece after firing. If a piece is 1 1/2" when made, it will be the size indicated by the 1 1/2 mark, shown at A. Thickness, construction and certain firing situations might have an impact on shrinkage.

Sometimes your question might be the other way around. Suppose you are making earrings that you want to be one inch in diameter after firing. To determine how large to make the initial PMC object, use the side of the ruler marked **Before Firing**. A piece that comes to the 1" mark (B) will shrink when fired to become an actual inch.

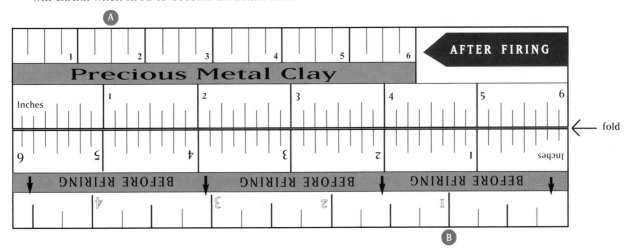

PMC+ / PMC 3 Ruler

The shrinkage of PMC+ and PMC 3 is about 12%, considerably less than standard PMC. Use the ruler below to help in estimating the shrinkage. The numbers in black are actual inches, while the red numbers indicate a reduction of 12%. This means that a pre-fired piece that measures 2", for instance, will be as large as the length indicated by the red 2.

Setting Heatproof Gems

Very few natural gemstones will stand the high temperatures required to fuse precious metal clays. Diamonds, sapphires, rubies and emeralds might, but tiny amounts of other minerals trapped inside the stones (inclusions) might cause them to discolor or crack. Fortunately for us, we live in a time when science has created a family of engineered materials called laboratory-grown gems.

These stones mimic the chemical ingredients and physical properties that went into the creation of stones in nature. They are manufactured at very high temperatures and therefore can safely withstand the stresses of being included in a PMC firing.

How can you tell if what you have is a lab-grown gem? The simplest and most reliable answer is to purchase what you need from a reputable dealer. Lapidary laboratories can perform tests to determine if a stone is genuine or manmade, but these are generally too costly to be practical. Another simple test is to try it. Set the stone inside the kiln when you're firing a batch of PMC. If it survives one firing, it will survive another. This risks the stone, but protects you from spending time on a PMC piece that will be ruined by a melted stone.

Every setting has unique properties, but here is a general description of the process of setting a stone. Modify this to create a setting that enhances both the stone and the object it adorns.

1. Allow enough material to curl over the edge of the stone and to insure that the stone will not stick out the back.

2. Determine the location of the stone and make a hole there, typically with a needle, a beverage stirrer or a drinking straw, depending on the size of the stone. This will make the setting more delicate in appearance.

3. Sometimes the PMC dries while you're working which can create an unattractive cracking around the edges where you press the stone into position. To avoid this, put a drop of water on the area and give it a minute to soak in. Lay the gem into place — I find that using tweezers makes this job a lot easier. Press straight down on the stone to seat it.

It's easy to visualize that the PMC will curl over the top of the stone as it shrinks, locking the stone into place. It's important to remember, though, that the same shrinkage is happening in the area beneath the stone. As the piece shrinks it will have the effect of squeezing the stone upward and out of the setting. To compensate for this, push the stone deeply into the PMC. As a rule of thumb, the PMC should be at least as high as the top of the table on a faceted stone.

4. If you are making a thin bezel, you'll need to compensate for shrinkage by working a little thicker, especially for standard PMC. If you start with a thin band, the bezel might tear as it shrinks. By providing sufficient thickness, the shrinkage will come from the thinning of the band.

5. Fire as recommended, then allow the piece to air cool. Use a burnisher, small files or a rubber-and-pumice abrasive wheel (no sandpaper) to smooth the rim of metal around the stone. Steel wool, scratchbrushes, tumbling shot and polishing compounds will not damage laboratory-grown stones.

Setting Heat-Sensitive Gems

Adding Settings Later

People with jewelrymaking experience can solder stone settings onto PMC pieces after they have been fired. Settings can be made in the studio as needed or purchased in standard sizes. These sterling or karat gold mountings can be soldered into place just as they would be when the object is fabricated or cast. Burnish the area to receive the solder and do not overheat.

Firing Sterling into PMC

The firing temperature of standard PMC will melt sterling, so settings should not be fired in place into that version. PMC+ and PMC3, on the other hand, can be fired at temperatures low enough to permit sterling elements to be pressed into the clay where they will fuse when fired. Be certain that the sterling element is clean of oil and tarnish. Provide a mechanical grip by filing or grinding grooves into the mounting so the silver clay will wrap itself physically onto it. Fire at temperatures no higher than 1470° F (800° C). Finish the piece like any other, then set the stone into the mounting. Use a bezel pusher, burnisher or pliers to force the prongs or bezel over the stone. Polish the area around the stone with a leather stick. This will enhance the look and also removes burs that might snag on clothing.

Making Bezels from PMC

It's possible to calculate the size before shrinkage so you can create a pocket that will be exactly the right size for the stone after the piece shrinks. This technique was used to make the piece on page 18.

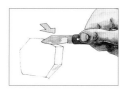

1. Trace the stone and calculate the pre-fired size by multiplying the dimensions by 1.28 for Standard PMC and 1.12 for PMC+ and PMC3. Use the paper pattern to cut out a strip for a wall that will eventually shrink to wrap the stone. Remember to compensate for shrinkage in height too. If the bezel wall is too high, it's usually not too difficult to file it down. If it's too short, you won't be able to set the gem.

2. Construct the piece, adding the wall in a way that incorporates the gem into the design of the whole. It might be necessary to add paste to the inside of the rim to attach the parts. This is okay, but do not add too much or the gem won't fit.

3. Mix plaster of Paris (available from hardware stores) and pour some into a paper cup to a thickness equivalent to the height of the bezel wall. Allow this to dry overnight, then carve it with a knife and file to exactly duplicate the shape of the stone. Set this into the bezel area and place the piece into the kiln.

4. Fire as recommended. As the PMC shrinks, it will come to rest against the plaster form. This will guarantee that even if your shrinkage calculations were a little off, the stone will still fit.

5. Finish the piece as usual, then set the stone into the bezel. If it is too tight, use burs or sandpaper to enlarge the space. Set the stone into place to check the height of the bezel. If it is too high, draw a guideline with a felt-tip pen, remove the stone and trim away excess with scissors or a file. Sand the edge to make it smooth and bright.

6. Return the stone to the mounting, then press the bezel wall against the gem to lock it into the piece. Push from all sides of the piece alternately, rather than starting at one point and working your way around. On a triangle or rectangle, start by pressing the corners. Smooth the bezel with files and polish with a burnisher or leather stick.

Firing Tips

Drying

The first step in transforming the clay-like PMC into a solid metal object is to drive off the moisture it contains. One way to do this is to simply set the finished piece aside to air dry. This can take anywhere from one hour to two days depending on thickness, how much water was added during modeling and local humidity.

Drying will be faster and more uniform when air can circulate around the piece. To lift it up off the table, set the finished work on a wad of paper towel or cloth, onto a sheet of foam rubber or onto a plastic mesh. This can be recycled from a berry container or made by gluing screen onto a frame. To speed up drying, use a hairdryer or put the piece in a low or moderate oven (200-300° F) for at least 15 minutes.

Precious Metal Clay can be fired in any sort of kiln that can attain and hold a temperature of 900° C /1650° F; (1000°C / 1830° F for gold). In practice this usually means a small electric kiln. If the piece is dry, the kiln can be brought up to temperature without delay. The rate of heating is called ramping speed. If the piece still contains a lot of water when put into the kiln — and especially if the piece is more than 1/8" (3 mm) thick — the ramp should be slow enough that the water has a chance to turn into steam and escape. This will happen in a kiln chamber that has reached 250° F (120° C). After 15 minutes at this temperature it is usually safe to heat up as fast as the kiln will go.

Firing Chart

		temperature		time
Standard PMC — silver		1650° F	900° C	two hours
Standard PMC — gold		1830°	1000°	two hours
PMC+ — silver		1650°	900°	10 minutes
	or	1560°	850°	20 minutes
	or	1470°	800°	30 minutes
PMC 3		1290°	700°	10 minutes
	or	1200°	650°	20 minutes
	or	1110°	600°	30 minutes

Firing Supports

Shelf Materials:
Setting work into a kiln and removing it after firing is a lot easier when the work is placed on some sort of tray or shelf.

- Bisque Tiles   These once-fired ceramic panels are inexpensive and available through ceramic supply companies. They are somewhat fragile and might break after a few firings.

- Soldering pads   Jewelry supply companies sell several brands of sheets used as soldering surfaces. These are more expensive than bisque tiles but last much longer.

- Soft firebrick   This is sold through ceramic supply companies. It can be cut with a hacksaw or wood saw to make slabs about an inch thick (thinner slabs will break).

- Terra cotta saucers   These are the bottom piece of the familiar red clay flowerpots sold in hardware and gardening stores. These are especially useful for volumetric (non-flat) pieces as described below.

Rounded Forms
Flat pieces can be set directly on a firing shelf, but rounded forms need to be supported. Use any of these powders as a support.

- Alumina hydrate   A white powder or granule used in ceramic studios.
- Vermiculite   A naturally occuring form of mica used as a soil additive. It is available from hardware stores and nurseries.
- Plaster of Paris   Use the powder as it comes from the bag — do not add water. This might pack itself into a lump during firing, but it can be easily broken apart.
- Investment   This is a plaster-based material used in jewelry casting.
- Grog   Fired and pulverized ceramic material that looks like sand.

These materials can be piled on the shelves described above, but the powders tend to spill off the edges. To contain the bedding material use a terracotta flower pot, a discarded saucer, or a carved-out fire brick.

SAFETY NOTE: *Any small particles can cause harm to the lungs and respiratory tract. Everyone should avoid breathing in dust and people with a history of breathing difficulty should be especially cautious.*

Matte Surfaces

Anyone who has eagerly opened a kiln door after a firing knows the odd feeling of seeing what look like whitewashed objects. Fresh out of the kiln, PMC doesn't look like silver at all but is a flat, matte white color. You might be surprised to learn that this is not a coating on the PMC, but is in fact the real color of silver. The reflective shine we usually think of is the result of the shape of the surface. The luster of silver is the reflection of ambient light.

If you could look at a cross section of fired PMC under a microscope, you'd see a semi-dense material with a top surface of countless peaks and valleys. If you envision the surface of velvet you'll have the right idea. Light falling on a surface like this becomes trapped — little bounces back — creating the visual effect of a matte surface. Polishing (of PMC or any material) is a matter of smoothing out the peaks and valleys so that most of the light bounces back.

Think of a continuum in which one end is totally matte (flat) and the other is highly reflective (shiny). Fresh out of the kiln, PMC is at the far end of this line; it can't get more matte. Left alone, it will stay this way, possibly discoloring slightly from dust or chemicals in the air, especially for areas in a design that are protected from contact, like the bottom of a groove. This bright white can provide an interesting contrast to polished silver.

As PMC is handled, the delicate surface will be compressed and the matte will be converted to a denser, reflective surface. This is usually a deliberate process (polishing) but it's also possible to allow a piece to become polished through wear. This is most relevant for objects that are handled or in contact with objects in the way a ring or key chain would be.

Butler Finish
When the butler gets caught up on his chores, the family silver has a warm delicate glow as a result of his hand-rubbed efforts. To achieve a finish that is not reflective but looks like silver, use any of the following techniques.

Steel Wool

Most hardware stores will sell steel wool, usually in the painting department. Use the finest available, designated as 4/0 or 0000. If available, nonferous bronze wool is even better and there is a new plastic version on the market that works well too. Rub any of these over the PMC in circular strokes. The longer and harder you rub, the shinier the piece will become. Rinse well in running water to remove all steel particles.

Pumice

Many hardware and paint supply stores sell a white powder that is made by pulverizing the soft expanded ash of volcanoes. Powdered pumice is used as a final finish in woodworking and has long been part of the jeweler's bag of tricks. Unlike some other finishing materials, pumice is chemically neutral — it's a kind of sand with no additives — and therefore it does not introduce grease or soap residue as it does its work.

Spill the pumice powder into a shallow dish so you can pick up more as you need it and allow it to fall back into the dish as you work. Rub the pumice across the surface of your work, either with your fingers or with a toothbrush. Pumice can be used either dry or mixed with water to make a paste. Adding water makes it a little easier to use, but the dry version gives a slightly brighter shine. Continue rubbing until you achieve the look you want. Pumice also works very well to remove liver of sulfur blackening from raised portions when you are patinating a work.

Scratchbushing

Jewelry supply companies sell a finishing tool called a scratchbrush that has bristles made of very thin brass or steel wires. Work over a dish of soapy water or at a sink, dipping the piece under a drizzle of water periodically. Put a little soap on the bristles, either by rubbing them with hand soap or with a few drops of liquid soap. Rub vigorously over the PMC, changing directions once in a while.

The piece will quickly disappear into a ball of lather, which is why you'll want to rinse it off periodically so you can check your progress. The more you brush, the brighter the shine will become, but brass brushing will not create a mirror-bright finish. Some designs look great when you use steel wool or a scratchbrush first over the whole piece, then follow up with a burnisher or polishing paper on selected areas.

Filing and Sanding

The great thing about PMC is that it's so easy to form. Often the work comes out of the firing needing only a little burnishing or scratchbrushing to be ready to use or wear. There are situations, though, when filing or sanding is needed to refine a shape. Sometimes I purposely stop working on a piece of PMC because it's so delicate I'm afraid to handle it any more than necessary. In those cases I prefer to smooth the piece after it is solid metal. And then of course, it can also happen that I change my mind about a design and want to alter the form or surface. For those cases, here's some basic information on files and sandpaper.

Any File Will Work

There are scores of shapes of files including many made for a particular material. Any will work to refine a PMC object. Pure silver is very soft so it will not damage any file, but heavy use might clog the teeth. Run a needle along the grooves of the file to clean it. Files cut on the push stroke and work best when the piece being filed is held firmly against a workbench.

Sandpaper Grit

The cutting power of sandpaper depends mostly on the abrasive material and the size of the particle. Silicon carbide is the hardest commonly available grit and the one preferred by most jewelers. Garnet and aluminum oxide will also work, but these papers will wear out faster when used on PMC. Abrasive papers are described by numbers which you'll find printed on the back (smooth) side. Start with a sandpaper coarse enough to work efficiently but not so rough it makes unwanted marks. Sometimes you'll use the whole sequence, from coarse to fine. If the task at hand is a minor reduction of an area that is already smooth, you might start with 320 then go to 400 and from there to a burnisher.

100s	Coarse	Changing the shape
200s	Medium	Removing textures, smoothing edges
300s	Medium/Fine	Removing scratches to prep for polishing
400s	Fine	Matte surface for a frosted shine; prep for scratchbrushing
600	Very Fine	Polishing paper

Sanding sticks

To increase leverage and make sandpaper easier to control, wrap a sheet of abrasive paper tightly around a flat piece of wood. Buy a piece of lattice at a lumber yard and cut it into one foot sections. Attach the sandpaper with tape or staples, using a scribe to crease each fold.

A variation on this is to glue strips of sandpaper to popsicle sticks, tongue depressors and dowels. This will offer a wide range of shapes and sizes. Emery boards are a useful and inexpensive option.

Salon boards, sold in the manicure department of drugstores, make terrific sanding sticks for PMC. They can be used on the material at any time during its life cycle: when green, when dried and after firing. They are available in several grits and are color-coded for easy identification.

Blackening Silver

Liver of Sulfur

This material is sold through jewelry suppliers as a yellow gravel. To use, dissolve a very small piece with very hot water to make an amber-colored liquid. Immerse the work and allow it to soak for about a minute. Remove the piece and rinse it well in running water. The piece can be left black or polished with any light abrasive like steel wool, baking soda, toothpaste, fine pumice, etc.

Silver Black, Black Max

These are acid-based proprietary solutions sold as ready-to-use liquids by jewelry suppliers. They are applied to the polished work with a brush or Q-Tip and work instantly. Rinse and dry the work, then remove the black color from the high spots by polishing with a cloth, toothpaste, steel wool or pumice.

Sequence

1. Fire the PMC as suggested by the manufacturer.
2. If necessary, refine the form by filing and sanding. Finish by tumbling, burnishing or scratchbrushing.
3. Darken with either of the above solutions. The liver of sulfur can take several minutes to achieve its full black effect, while the proprietary versions (which contain a mild acid) work immediately. In both cases, follow the coloring process with a rinse in running water.
4. It's difficult to darken jewelry selectively, so the usual method is to make the whole piece black then polish away the black layer where the high shine is desired. Remove black with polishing paper, fine pumice powder or a polishing stick with compound. To achieve a mirror finish, follow this by rubbing forcefully with a rouge cloth.

Usually most of the patina is polished off so the black remains only in the recesses. For an alternate look, try making an object shiny-black all over. First polish the piece to a high shine, then darken it as described above. Leave the work in the liver of sulfur solution for several minutes to develop a thick sulfide layer. Tumble this for 5-10 minutes then dry it with a soft cloth. The effect is a shiny black like polished hematite or steel. If you don't like it, either rub off the black with fine sandpaper or reheat the PMC to burn off the patina.

Polishing By Hand

When light hits a smooth surface, most of it is bounced back into a viewer's eye and we perceive the object as "shiny" (think of a car). If the surface is irregular, some of the light is trapped and we perceive the object as "not shiny" (think of a wool blanket). To make something shiny we make its surface smooth. In some materials, like wood or stone, we can only do this by cutting off the projecting bits with grinding and sanding equipment. When a material is malleable like metal, we have the additional option of pressing the raised areas down. This process is known as burnishing and can be done alone or in conjunction with abrasion.

The key to achieving a mirror-like polish is to follow the correct sequence to the correct degree. In other words, move from one step to the next in logical progression without skipping or abbreviating any step. This will often run from coarse papers, through four or five grits to get to a high-numbered paper, but bear in mind that no two pieces will be handled exactly the same. Depending on the shape of the piece and the intended finish, you may start the process at any point on the continuum.

Traditional Abrasive Papers

For centuries, soft stones were rubbed against metal objects to wear down sharp edges and make the surface flat. The dust from these stones (a.k.a. sand) was rubbed along the metal with fingers or with a bit of leather or cloth. As paper and adhesives became available, sandpaper as we think of it today came into use.

Abrasive papers have three components: grit, vehicle and binder. The grit can be a naturally occuring or a manmade substance. The best choices are tough particles that either resist breaking or break in such a way that they form sharp edges. The vehicle is the carrier that presses the grit against the material being finished, in this case paper. Modern developments have introduced waterproof papers and plastic films, both of which have some advantages over conventional paper. In the case of paper, a thin glue is used to cement particles onto the sheet.

Grit Size

Abrasive papers are identified by the size of the mesh used to sort the particles — the higher the number, the finer the grit. Different materials are used for the "sand" of sandpaper. Garnet and aluminum oxide will work on PMC, but silicon carbide is

100s   200s   300s   400s

preferred. Most hardware and paint stores will sell 100 grit through 400 grit and this will get you started. For polishing you'll need to go to at least 600 grit, available from some hardware stores, and then go into specialty abrasives sold by jewelry suppliers and some auto parts stores.

Finishing Papers

A recent development in abrasives has created papers with particles that are so small and so uniform they can create a mirror polish. These are available under several brand names in a variety of styles from jewelry supply companies. In some versions the standard grit designations have been replaced by the actual dimension of the particles, measured in microns. In this case, the lower numbers are finer papers. Move in sequence from coarse to fine, skipping none and using each paper until the marks of the preceding stage have been removed.

Polishing Compounds

As the progression moves from coarse to fine, the particles keep getting smaller until they become too tiny to glue to a paper backing. For centuries the solution was to mix the "sand" with wax or grease that could be rubbed into a fabric backing. These mixtures are called polishing compounds. A glance at a jewelry supply catalog will reveal dozens of compounds, each with its proponents. We'll look at a few of the classics, but you might want to experiment with others. The description that follows about how to use compounds applies to all varieties.

- Bobbing   A coarse relatively aggressive compound used to round edges, remove scratches and alter shapes slightly.

- White Diamond   A fast cutter that simultanously leaves a bright shine.

- Rouge   A polishing compound that brings out the warmth and richness in silver. It does not remove scratches.

To use compounds by hand, rub them into a piece of leather or a durable fabric like denim, canvas or twill. See page 113 for information about polishing sticks you can make yourself. Rub the compound into the fabric to make an even layer. These same compounds can be used for machine polishing, as described on the next page.

Machine Polishing

If you think it's necessary to have a buffing machine to achieve a mirror bright finish on silver, read the preceding page. It's not. If you have a buffing machine or flexible shaft device and are wondering if this can be used on PMC, the answer is yes.

Polishing is a process of evening a surface by either cutting off or pressing down the high spots. The cutting is done by dragging hard particles ("sand") across the surface, a process that can be done with elbow grease or a well-oiled motor.

A buffing or polishing machine (sometimes called a polishing lathe) is a $1/4$ horsepower or larger motor that is mounted on a tabletop and designed to spin wheels made of fabric or felt. These are potentially dangerous because of the risk of getting clothing or hair tangled in the spinning axle. Always keep long hair and loose clothing tied back. Also, abrasive particles will be thrown up from the wheel, so eye protection is critical. It is outside the scope of this book to provide full instructions on the use of equipment. If you have not received instruction from a qualified instructor, seek detailed information from a reliable source.

A flexible shaft machine, or flex shaft for short, is a miniature version of the buffing machine. The same safety rules apply but because the motor and accessories are much smaller, the risks are reduced. Other advantages of the flex shaft are its portability and the wide range of tasks it can accomplish, like sanding and drilling. A flex shaft machine consists of three parts: a small high-speed motor, a variable-speed foot pedal and a cylindrical handpiece attached to a hose-like shaft. These machines are available through jewelry supply companies and cost around $250.

Sanding and Buffing Wheels

The first step is to achieve the desired form and surface, typically through filing and sanding. This can be done by motor or by hand. The flexible shaft is better suited to this task than the stationary buffing machine because it allows you to swivel the tools over the metal piece. A huge array of sanding and grinding wheels are commercially available, some permanently mounted on shafts (mandrels) and others made to snap or screw onto rods. Experimentation is your best bet here. Purchase a sampling to determine which wheels are best suited to your forms and working methods.

The polishing wheels for motorized equipment fall into two large categories: hard and soft. Hard wheels are made of felt and have the advantage of allowing increased pressure and the ability to localize contact. That is, you can steer them to just where you want them and press down hard. Soft wheels are made of layers of fabric that have been stitched together. Depending on the kind of fabric and the method of stitching, these vary a little in their effect. Generally, they round edges and leave a bright shine. The same sorts of wheels are available for full-size motors and flexible shaft uses, the only difference being their size.

Compounds

As purchased, polishing wheels are like sandpaper with no sand. They need to be impregnated with abrasive or polishing compound. Again, there are many to choose from and experimentation is suggested. The traditional favorite for removing scratches is tripoli, but its modern cousins, White Diamond and ZAM among others are gaining popularity.

With the wheel turning, touch the compound to either felt or muslin for a few seconds to charge the wheel. Wear goggles because this abrasive powder is about to be distributed around the work area. Keep the tool moving over the surface of the piece and approach from a variety of angles to avoid wearing a groove. When finished, wash the work in soapy water with a little ammonia added.

Using Epoxy

Epoxy is a thermosetting plastic with strong adhesive properties. In other words, epoxy is really strong glue. Not long ago, epoxy was a technological marvel, but now it can be found in any hardware store. Epoxies are available in many types, the principle differences being color and setting time.

All epoxies are sold in two parts, typically called resin and hardener. When these elements are joined, they set off a chain reaction that converts the two liquids into a tough solid mass. In order for the epoxy to harden to its a potential, it is important that the two parts are very well blended.

Use

Epoxy is great stuff, but it can live up to high expectations only when handled properly. Problems with adhesives are not usually the fault of the glue but the result of ignoring a few simple rules.

1. Surfaces must be clean

Remove dirt, oil, grease, soap — everything — before using any glue. Just because a surface doesn't look dirty doesn't mean that it is chemically clean.

2. Provide a rough surface

Even the strongest adhesive can have trouble sticking to slick surfaces. Wherever possible, file or sand the surfaces to be glued. This has the added advantage of scraping away dirt and oil.

3. Follow the manufacturer's directions

Because glue is so simple, we sometimes take it for granted. Read the directions on the package carefully and follow them exactly. Temperature and proportion are critical. Accuracy here can make the difference between a joint that holds for five minutes and one that holds for five years.

Mix equal parts by squeezing out lines of equal length.

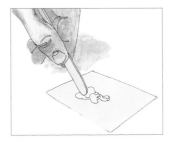

Mix the parts thoroughly, spinning the paper as you work so the mix is uniform.

Hanging Beads as Drops

There's something special about jewelry that moves. As sparkling silver and brightly colored gems swing, they catch the light and animate the piece. Pieces of jewelry with dangles exaggerate the movements of the wearer and catch our attention.

Head pins are lengths of silver wire that have a small disk on one end. They are available from jewelry supply and bead shops, usually for only a few cents each. Slide your bead (or beads) onto the pin. Test to be sure they don't fall off. If the hole in your bead is too large, use a washer or smaller bead first. The drop will look best if the loop at the top is close to the bead, centered and not too large. Here are two ways to complete the hanging loop.

Simple Version

Snip the wire to a length equal to three times the diameter of the intended loop. In other words, a 1/8" loop will use 3/8" of wire. Cut with wire snips or toenail clippers.

Grasp the tip of the wire with round-nose pliers and roll your hand in a single motion to wrap the wire around the tip. Use the place on the jaws that matches the intended loop: small loops are wrapped near the tip and larger loops will use the area closer to the joint. Go as far as you can, which will probably take you about three-fourths of the way around.

Pull the pliers out and get a new grip, using the tip of the pliers to hold the wire just below the loop. Bend the loop backward slightly to make it more centered over the shaft. Reinsert the pliers into the loop and roll it one more time to close the loop.

To keep the eyelet round, open it with a sideways twist when attaching the drop.

Wrapped Version

This style uses more wire than you might think — be cautious about snipping any material off. Slide the bead onto a head pin and grab the wire with round-nose pliers at the point where the loop will be when done. Pull the wire around the pliers three-fourths of the way. At the end of this step, the free end should be sticking out at a right angle to the shaft.

Wrap the wire around the length of the head pin, taking pains to lay each twist tightly against the preceding wrap. The last bit of wire is the hardest to move. Use flat-jawed pliers to lay the final bit down as tightly as possible, then snip off whatever excess sticks out.

Ornamental

Bend a wire into a spiral to hold the bead from below.

Tie a knot in a wire, using two pairs of pliers to pull it tight. Snip off one end to make the head.

Embed a head pin into an ornament made of PMC+ or PMC3. Fire at the lowest possible temperature, then finish as usual.

Using Cords

Basic Jump Ring

Slide a metal ring (called a jump ring) onto the cord, double over the end and tie it with thread. This might be the same color as the cord or you might use a contrasting color as a highlight. Tie off the end and seal it with glue or clear nail polish, then snip away any loose ends. Add a spring ring, safety clasp or lobster-claw clasp.

Comercial End Caps

Machine-made end caps are available from jewelry supply and bead companies. They are attached with a strong glue like epoxy, which is sold in hardware stores. Don't use cyano-acrylate (SuperGlue) because it does not work well on porous materials like fabric.

In the simplest cases you mix the glue, gather a drop on the end of the cord and press it into place. If the cord is fraying (which makes it difficult to insert) or if it is too small for the cap, try this trick: Wrap a piece of tape tightly around the cord an inch or two from the end (this is easier than working right at the tip). It also helps to have a friend pull the cord tight while you do this. Cut the cord through the tape at a place where the wrap will be hidden in the cap and glue as described above.

PMC End Caps

It's often a good idea to make cord ends that relate to the pendant or necklace. Select a rod that is a bit larger than the cord you will use, to allow for shrinkage. Make a tube of PMC+ or PMC3 — either of these will allow for a sterling wire to be fired in place. Cap the tube shape with a small sheet and seal the edges, then press a sterling or gold loop into place. Fire as recommended and polish.

Over-the-Head Necklace

You won't need a clasp when the cord is long enough to be slipped over the wearer's head. To make a tidy joint on a thick cord (like leather) use a sharp knife to slice an angle on each end. This will allow the cord to overlap without making a bulky lump. Glue the overlap and temporarily bind the joint with tape. When the glue has set, remove the tape and wrap neatly with thread or thin metal wire. It's also possible to make a cylinder of precious metal clay. Cut an opening along the axis, then fire and polish it. Glue the cord ends together, set the cylinder in position and squeeze it closed with pliers. This will cover the joint in the cord and add a decorative element at the same time.

Assorted Bails

The term bail is used to describe the loop or eyelet that allows a pendant to be hung from a chain. The most basic version of a bail is a hole and while this works, it forces the pendant to hang sideways. The simplest effective bail is a hole with a loop of wire in it.

All worthwhile solutions have these things in common:
- allow the pendant to hang straight and unencumbered
- are secure
- relate to both pendant and cord, either by coordinating them or by making a clear break between the two parts
- do not overpower the pendant

This page shows a few of the gazillion ways you can bridge the space between a pendant and cord. Many of these solutions are used in projects in the early part of this book.

Thread a sterling loop through a hole in a PMC pendant.   Use a sterling, brass, or copper wire to make a bail by wrapping it around itself.

Make a "handle" of PMC in the original design, fire flat, then bend around to make a loop.   A sterling strip can be attached with a rivet pin after firing.

A PMC ornament is used as a rivet pin to hold a bail made of sterling.    Similar to the example above, but in this case the bail is ornamental and made from PMC.

A curved piece of sterling sheet can be fused into PMC+ or PMC3, or soldered onto any version of PMC.   Here a sterling tube is fused onto a PMC+ or PMC3 pendant, or soldered after firing onto a piece made in any version of PMC.

Part Three
Tools You Can Make

Textured Rolling Pins

Here's an idea that's too good to pass up. For only a few pennies and the investment of less than a half hour's time, you can make a collection of tools that are versatile, easy to use and efficient. This page presents three alternate methods of making textured rolling pins and you will probably come up with some ideas of your own.

Incised Design

1. Cut a convenient length of PVC or similar plastic pipe.

2. Draw a design on the pipe in pencil or ink.

3. Carve into the plastic with a linoleum cutter, graver or similar tool. Remember that the image pressed into the PMC will be the reverse of what you cut. This usually doesn't matter with a graphic pattern, but it is important when printing letters, numbers or specific icons.

4. Rub steel wool or Scotch-Brite over the surface to break off burs.

5. Roll out a sheet of PMC with a smooth roller to make a slab a little thicker than your intended result. Switch to the textured roller and make a single pass to create a clean impression.

6. As described, and assuming your carving tools are sharp, this roller will create a crisp raised pattern. If the design calls for a gentler, worn look, rub the pipe with sandpaper to round over the edges.

Raised Pattern

1. Cut a convenient length of PMC pipe or similar tubing. A section of wooden dowel can also be used for this tool.

2. Scrape the pipe with a blade or rub it with sandpaper to remove surface oils. This will simultaneously create a coarse surface on the plastic that will help the applied layer of polymer to stick.

3. Paint a layer of acrylic glue like Sobo, Elmer's or acrylic medium onto the tube with a brush, a Q-Tip, or a finger. Allow it to dry.

4. Create the desired pattern by applying polymer clay onto the tube. Roll out a thick sheet and wrap it around the rod. Cut off excess and press the ends together until they are well knit and have no raised joint.

5. The polymer layer can be textured, carved or in any other way given a pattern. Use a polymer tool, kitchen utensil, art material or found object that makes an interesting shape.

6. Bake the roller in a toaster oven as recommended by the manufacturer to harden the polymer clay. It will probably be bound tight to the rod, but if it becomes loose, glue it down with epoxy.

Found Textures

1. Condition enough polymer clay to make a rod that will be about 3/4" in diameter and long enough to be convenient. This might be as short as 3" or as long as 6" depending on the scale of your work. Work the rod in your hands or through a pasta machine to make it soft, then roll it into a solid rod.

2. Roll the rod firmly against a textured surface. Examples include weathered wood, coarse fabrics, cement, bark, lace, etc. Elements that are raised in the found object will be recessed in your roller. When you use this on PMC, you'll have a raised texture again. Follow that? Of course, because of shrinkage, the PMC piece will have a sharper, smaller version of the texture.

3. Pick up textures from rocks, trees, buildings, concrete, leaves, bark, toys, etc. Once you get used to it, you'll find yourself always on the lookout for interesting textures to capture and bring back to the studio. In addition to their aesthetic value, you might find that you select certain textures for symbolic or personal reasons.

Rubber Stamps

Because PMC is soft, even rubber stamps can be used to make impressions and designs. Stamps are sold in toy stores, stationery shops and art supply stores.

In addition to commercial stamps you can make your own. Put aside your usual notions about what tools are made of and you might be surprised at what you come up with...

Make your own permanent stamps by cutting a rubber eraser with a razor knife. Remember to carve the image "backwards" — the mirror image — of the mark you want to make in PMC.

Don't feel restricted to the stamp as it appears. Press the stamp into PMC, then cut the slab into pieces and collage them together, perhaps splicing in additional smooth and patterned pieces.

What's picture to some is pattern to others. Use multiple impressions of several stamps to make a texture. Vary the density to create interesting contrast.

PMC stamps can also be made of wood, polymer clay, metal or ceramic. Even simple shapes can make attractive borders and patterns when used in combination.

Drill Bit Handles

Here's one of those "How did I ever get along without it" ideas. It's about as simple as dirt and, like many simple ideas, elegant and practical.

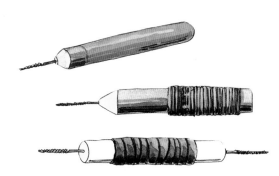

1. Buy a wooden dowel at a hardware store and cut it into pencil-sized pieces.

2. Select several of your most useful size drill bits. The chart below shows the sizes I find most useful.

3. Drill a hole in the end of a dowel, one for each bit. Be sure the bit is aligned with the axis of the rod.

4. Epoxy the bits into place.

5. To make a fancy grip on each tool (and this is entirely optional), wind a cord around the dowel. If these are of different colors or lengths the drills will be easy to tell apart. Of course you could also finish the handle with paint or tape, or do nothing at all.

6. Use these tools on green (unfired) or finished PMC to enlarge and smooth holes.

Popular Drill Bit Sizes

Drill #	Inches	mm	B&S
46	5/64	2.0	12
43	3/32	2.6	11
51	1/16	1.6	14
55	3/64	1.2	17
65	1/32	0.8	20
70		0.64	22

Pierced Matrix

This page is dedicated to metalsmiths and anyone who has a metalsmith friend they can persuade to help them. This technique is a bit time-consuming in the initial step, but yields a permanent template.

1. Lay out the intended design so it can be pierced into sheet metal. I like to use an adhesive-backed material called "Crack-n-Peel" — a large name tag or mailing label works well. Because you will be piercing all the way through, you do not need to compensate for a reverse image. Cut out a "right side" image, then flip the sheet over to get the reverse.

2. If the design was drawn in pencil, trace over it in ink so it won't smudge. Clean a sheet of 18- or 20-gauge brass, copper or nickel silver by scouring it with Scotch Brite or sandpaper. Apply the pattern.

3. Centerpunch a tiny crater in each compartment of the design and drill a hole. Insert a sawblade and pierce out the shapes using standard metalsmithing techniques.

4. When all piercing is finished, remove the paper by burning or with a solvent like nail polish remover. Scour the surface with Scotch Brite, steel wool or sandpaper to remove burs and slightly round the edges.

5. Set a slab of PMC on the matrix and roll it lightly — lift the clay to check the results. Alternately, set the metal matrix onto a sheet of PMC and press or roll it.

6. Variation: Form the pierced sheet into a cylinder and roll it across a slab of PMC. For intricate designs, solder the pierced sheet into a metal base to prevent distortion when bending.

Polishing Sticks

Don't you love it when your favorite tools are inexpensive and easy to make? Here's a tool I depend on to achieve crisp, highly polished surfaces. For more information about the use of this tool, turn to page 100.

1. At a lumber yard or builders supply store, buy a strip of lattice. This is a specific cut of knot-free pine about 1 1/4" wide and 1/4" thick. Alternatively, use a ruler or section of yardstick.

2. Next you'll need a piece of leather to glue onto the wood. Of course you can buy this from a leather company, but an alternate source is to get a belt or a handbag from a second-hand store.

3. Mix up some epoxy and spread a thin, even coat on the wood. Press the leather and wood together and use a stack of books or similar weight to press the parts together as the glue sets.

4. Trim off excess leather with a razor knife.

5. Rub polishing compound like rouge, White Diamond, ZAM, etc. into the leather. Compounds are available from jewelry supply and auto part companies.

6. Use this polishing stick after the finest grade of sandpaper to create a mirror-like finish.

Cookie Cutters

You'll find a wide range of metal and plastic silhouette dies (a.k.a. cookie cutters) to use with PMC. Sooner or later, though, you'll want something that is either not available or made only in the wrong size. Experienced metalworkers will quickly see how they can make the cutters from copper, brass or nickel silver using standard silver soldering techniques. This page is intended for readers whose only metalworking experience involves a can opener and whose only tools are household scissors and pliers.

1. Eat food. Specifically, eat food from smooth-walled tin cans. This does not include soda cans (too thin) or others that are manufactured with corrugated ridges.

2. Draw the silhouette of your cutter, remembering to account for the shrinkage of PMC. You might be able to trace your outline from a book and use a photocopier to adjust the size. Measure the silhouette with a wire to determine the length of metal needed to make the die. Add 1/2" to this length.

3. Remove both the top and the bottom from a clean can, then cut at the seam with kitchen scissors. BE CAREFUL — the edges are sharp! It's a good idea to wear work gloves. Cut off the thick bands at the top and bottom to leave a panel of plain, flat metal. Recut one edge if necessary to get a straight line.

4. Cut a strip of metal with parallel edges to make the cutter. This will probably be 1/4" to 1/2" wide depending on the overall size of the shape you are making. Smooth the strip to make it straight and even.

5. Bend the strip into shape by working directly on your drawing. Use pliers to make sharp bends and your fingers to make curves. This isn't quite as easy as it sounds, so you might want to cut an extra strip and practice a few bends before you start on your shape. As you work, check often to be sure the strip always lies flat on the table.

6. Measure so that there is enough length to overlap the ends about a quarter of an inch. Make a cut in each end, halfway across the width of the strip, starting from the top on one side and from the bottom on the other. Interlock these to close the form. This joint can be sealed with epoxy or soft solder to reinforce the cutter.

Wooden Tweezers

As you work with smaller and smaller pieces, you'll find that the same fingers that seemed fine holding a spoon at breakfast have become as clumsy as sausages. What you need to do miniature work are miniature fingers — and that's just what tweezers are. Standard steel tweezers from the medicine chest or jewelry studio will be fine with PMC, but they are sharper and heavier than needed. This version is gentle on clay and more consistent with the delicate feel of the process. An additional advantage is that by making these tweezers yourself you have the ability to customize the shape for specific needs.

1. Select two smooth straight popsicle sticks. These are available:
   a) by eating a popsicle
   b) from a craft supply store (ask for craft sticks).

2. Whittle, saw or file a gradual point on one end of each stick.

3. File or sand a slope on the other end as shown. This should be a flat plane. To test the angle, press the stick onto the tabletop. The area under your finger should touch the table firmly (it shouldn't rock). The angle should be such that three or four coins will just fit under the tip. Repeat identically for both legs of the tweezers.

4. Spread a thin film of white glue on the sloped areas of both pieces, set them together and clamp them in a bulldog clamp. Allow to dry for at least several hours.

5. Remove the clamp and test the tweezers. Pinch the tips together and file or sand the point to whatever shape will best suit your needs.

Extruder

In its moldable form, PMC is too thick to press through a syringe. It's possible to thin the PMC with water to make a paste consistency. This can be extruded with normal hand pressure, but the resulting thread will quickly sag out of shape because of the extra water. The manufacturer was aware of this so they created a special consistency that can be forced through a nozzle and retain its shape. The device on this page shows a do-it-yourself extruder made from standard supplies available from a well-stocked hardware store. This tool uses the Archimedian principal of a screw mechanism to increase leverage.

List of Supplies

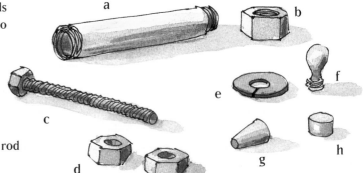

a   Brass pipe, 3" x 3/8" – threaded on both ends
b   1/4" Compression nuts – these should fit onto the ends of the pipe (you'll need 2)
c   1/4" x 4" Fine-thread bolt
d   1/4" Brass nuts to fit the bolt (you'll need 2)
e   1/4" Lock washer
f   Brass knurled nut (lamp supplies)
g   Cake tip (might need to be cut down)
h   Plug — polymer clay or a section of a metal rod

Construction Details

Slide the brass knurled nut all the way onto the bolt and secure it there by adding the lock washer and a nut. Screw this tightly together.

Solder the other brass nut onto the top of one of the compression fittings. This is the only part of the project that requires silver soldering — if you can't do it yourself you might be able to persuade a jewelrymaker to help you.

The shape of the extruded thread is determined by the nozzle (g). These can be purchased where cake decorating supplies are sold or improvised from pen tips, toys and tools. Cut as needed to fit inside the compression fitting.

When the pipe is filled with PMC the bolt will press into it with great force. Because the threaded rod doesn't completely fill up the interior space, the PMC will try to squirt around it. To prevent this, you will need to insert a plug. This is a cylinder about a half inch long that makes a snug fit on the inside of the tube. It can be made by filing a bit of steel rod to the correct size, or by firing a bit of polymer clay in place. Coat a small lump of clay with cornstarch (to prevent sticking) and force it into the pipe. Bake at 275° F for 30 minutes. Use a small metal disk on top of the polymer plug to give it extra strength.

To Use
Unscrew the back end and insert a rod of PMC in the pipe. Cap it with the plug and screw the bolt section into place — finger pressure is enough. Turn the bolt until the PMC starts to come out the tip. To set aside briefly, seal the loaded extruder in a plastic bag to prevent drying. When done for the day, the PMC should be removed and the tool cleaned.

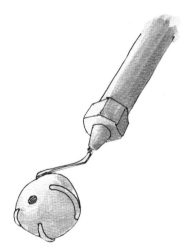

Cleaning
If you are using the extruder regularly, seal it in an air-tight bag with a small bit of damp-ened paper towel. This will preserve the moisture in the clay. If you are done, or won't be using the extruder for several days, squirt out the unused clay and clean the pipe with a wet cloth. Though it might seem a bit tedious, this process is much easier now than after the clay has dried.

Special thanks to Dana Carlson for help on this.

Tumbler

List of Parts

a   Rectangular plastic ware
     (e.g. Rubbermaid 3.2 qt. Servin' Saver #3901)

b   Nalgene water bottle

c   3 feet 1/2" PVC pipe

d   Epoxy or similar glue

e   2 feet of 5/16 or 1/4" threaded rod

f   8 bolts for the rod

g   4 washers

h   Electric drill (or small variable speed motor)
     Several rubber bands

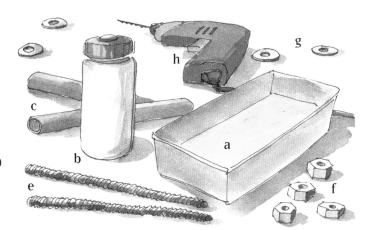

Preparing the Bottle

1. Cut the strap that connects the lid to the jar.

2. Cut two lengths of pipe to the same length as the inside flat portion of the walls.

3. Slice the pipe along its length with a saw. Trim the edges by scraping them with a knife.

4. Glue three of the four half-pipe pieces into the bottle. These are necessary to make the shot cascade over the work. Without them the shot would simply slide along the sides and not create the burnishing effect.

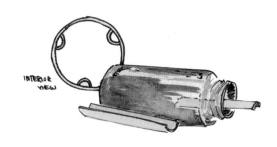

INTERIOR VIEW

Making the Base

1. The plastic dish provides two low walls that are parallel and a fixed distance apart. An alternative could be made by screwing two small pieces of wood onto a base. Drill holes for the threaded rod in the narrow end of the container, near the top. Measure to be sure the holes are all the same distance from the edge; this will insure that the rods are level.

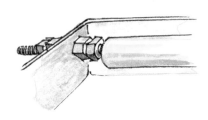

2. Cut a length of PVC pipe so that it fits into the opening of the plastic container with about 3/4" to spare.

3. Screw two nuts onto one of the rods and tighten them against each other. This will lock the nuts into position and prevent them from traveling as the device vibrates.

4. Insert the rod through one of the holes, slide a washer on next, then slip the pipe onto the rod. Put another washer on after the pipe.

5. Slide the threaded rod as needed to get it into position and screw a pair of nuts onto the end. The idea is that the rod is securely fastened into the container and the pipe is able to rotate freely.

6. Wrap several rubber bands around the other rod at two places equidistant from the center to make traction bearings. Slide this rod into the plasticware and screw on two pairs of nuts to hold it into the container. This rod must be allowed to rotate freely and should project out at one end long enough to connect to the motor. The motor will turn this rod, which in turn causes the jar to rotate.

Set Up

1. Small motors can be purchased from industrial suppliers or recycled from small appliances. An alternative is to use a variable speed electric drill. These can be purchased at discount chain stores for about $20. For the seriously cash-challenged, the mechanism could probably be modified to run on hamsterpower.

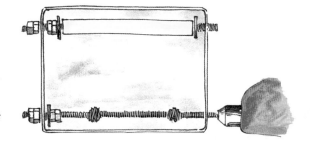

2. Though perhaps not necessary when using a drill, there is some advantage in connecting the drive element to the box. Screwing the plastic ware container onto a sheet of plywood or wide board will make the whole arrangement stronger. Depending on the heights of the units, it might be necessary to shim the motor or drill on a small piece of wood or Styrofoam to bring it up to be level with the shaft.

3. Put steel shot and tumbling compound into the bottle, ideally at least half full. In theory any polished steel parts can be substituted for commercial shot, so if you have a cheap source of ball bearings, polished nails or other miscellany, you might want to experiment. For more information about commercially available shot and solution, see page 124.

4. Connect the parts and run the motor on its slowest possible speed. Set the bottle (with the lid tightly screwed on) into position between the rods. It should rotate with a majestic motion.

Special thanks to Nicole Bsullak for help on this.

Health & Safety

It seems like every time we pick up the newspaper we learn of a new threat to our health. What a pleasure to find out that Precious Metal Clay will never make news that way. PMC has been certified by an independent testing facility to be safe in every phase of its use and to conform to ASTM D4236. This means that it is safe to handle and does not cause any threat to users, their children or pets.

Handling

PMC is about as dangerous as bread dough. The materials of which it is made contain nothing toxic or even strong. I wouldn't recommend putting it in your mouth (an expensive snack), but there is nothing poisonous in PMC. If you choose to use sharp blades or needles with PMC, be careful about cuts and stabs.

Firing

As described elsewhere in this book, firing often includes support materials like firebrick, soldering pads, alumina hydrate and other refractory powders. Like all fine particles, these pose a risk, particularly for people with respiratory problems. It is not that the materials themselves are harmful, but rather that the small size of the particles allows them to lodge in the membranes of the respiratory track. It is common sense to avoid stirring up dust whenever possible and to avert your face if a puff of dust is accidentally created. People with known respiratory problems should consider wearing a respirator or dust mask.

When PMC is heated in a kiln, the binder burns away, typically around $700°$ F ($371°$ C). This causes a small amount of smoke that has a characteristic "burned toast" odor. This is not dangerous, but some people might find the odor disagreeable. If the kiln is contained, the smoke and smell are largely trapped inside and are vaporized as the kiln reaches higher temperatures. If your kiln has a hole, this can be plugged by carving a conical plug from firebrick or plaster to reduce the smoke that is released into the room and minimize the odor.

The high temperature of firing suggests that care must be taken around the kiln. Think of everything your mother told you as a child about playing near the kitchen stove and increase it threefold. Kilns are usually well insulated, but take care that they are safely removed from combustibles like paper towels, curtains or wooden walls. Be sure that the cord is located safely away from foot traffic so it is impossible for someone to trip on the cord in passing. The ideal arrangement calls for a heatproof surface like bricks in front of the kiln on which to place work as it is withdrawn. Always wear gloves and long sleeves to protect your hands and arms when reaching into the kiln.

To protect against the risk of shock, always turn off a kiln before reaching in with tweezers or tongs. If these were to touch the elements, a severe shock might result.

Finishing

After firing, PMC is fine silver, a material so benign that it is used in dental fillings and medical implants. The materials used to finish silver are not quite so kind. Polishing compounds such as tripoli, White Diamond, rouge, etc. are small particles and deserve the same care mentioned above. Again, it's not that the compounds themselves are chemically dangerous, but that any small particle can become lodged in the lungs. As before, avoid stirring up dust and wear a mask if you are aware of a problem.

Melting Points

It's often helpful to know the relative melting points of materials. This makes it possible to predict what metals can be fired together and which materials will not withstand the heat of firing. In cases where variations are possible depending on manufacturers' alloys, the figures are shown in italics.

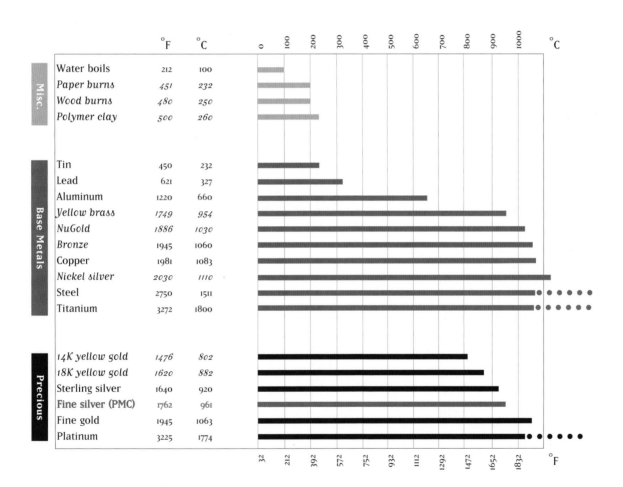

		°F	°C
Misc.	Water boils	212	100
	Paper burns	*451*	*232*
	Wood burns	*480*	*250*
	Polymer clay	*500*	*260*
Base Metals	Tin	450	232
	Lead	621	327
	Aluminum	1220	660
	Yellow brass	*1749*	*954*
	NuGold	*1886*	*1030*
	Bronze	*1945*	*1060*
	Copper	1981	1083
	Nickel silver	*2030*	*1110*
	Steel	2750	1511
	Titanium	3272	1800
Precious	*14K yellow gold*	*1476*	*802*
	18K yellow gold	*1620*	*882*
	Sterling silver	1640	920
	Fine silver (PMC)	1762	961
	Fine gold	1945	1063
	Platinum	3225	1774

Relative Sizes

B & S	mm	decimal inches	fractional inches	drill size
0	8.5	.325	21/64	
1	7.35	.289	9/32	
2	6.5	.258	1/4	
3	5.83	.229	7/32	1
4	5.19	.204	13/64	6
5	4.62	.182	3/16	15
6	4.11	.162	5/32	20
7	3.67	.144	9/64	27
8	3.26	.129	1/8	30
9	2.91	.114		
10	2.59	.102		38
11	2.30	.091	3/32	43
12	2.05	.081	5/64	46
13	1.83	.072		50
14	1.63	.064	1/16	51
15	1.45	.057		52
16	1.29	.051		54
17	1.15	.045	3/64	55
18	1.02	.040		56
19	0.912	.036		60
20	0.813	.032	1/32	65
21	0.724	.029		67
22	0.643	.025		70
23	0.574	.023		71
24	0.511	.020		74
25	0.455	.018		75
26	0.404	.016	1/64	77
27	0.361	.014		78
28	0.330	.013		79
29	0.279	.011		80
30	0.254	.010		

Resources

Organisations

The Crafts Council   0207/278-7700
44a Pentonville Road   0207/837-6891 fax
Islington, London, N1 9BY
www.craftscouncil.org.uk

The Goldsmiths' Company   0207/606-7010
Goldsmiths Hall   0207/606-1511
Foster Lane
London, EC2V 6BN
www.thegoldsmiths.co.uk

Mid Cornwall School of Jewellery   01726/817-989
Treesmill Farm
Treesmill
Tywardreath, Par
Cornwall, PL24 2TX
www.mcsj.co.uk
lisa@mcsj.co.uk

PMC Guild UK   01726/816-600
PO Box 219
Par, PL25 9AP
www.pmcguild.co.uk
director@pmcguild.co.uk

Magazines of interest to PMC artists

Bead & Button
PO Box 1612   262/796-8776
Waukesha, WI 53187-1612   262/796-1615 fax
USA
www.beadandbutton.com

Lapidary Journal
300 Chsterfield Parkway   610/232-5700
Suite 100
Malvern, PA 19355
USA
www.lapidaryjournal.com

Metalsmith
Society of North American
   Goldsmiths (SNAG)   541/345-5689
540 Oak Street   541/345-1123 fax
Suite A, Eugene
OR 97401
USA
www.snagmetalsmith.org
info@snagmetalsmith.org

Ornament
PO Box 452   800/888-8950
Mt. Morris, IL 61054-0452
USA
www.ornamentmagazine.com

Studio PMC
PMC Guild UK   01726/816-600
PO Box 219
Par, PL25 9AP
www.pmcguild.co.uk
director@pmcguild.co.uk

Art Jewelry magazine
Kalmbach Publishing Co.   262/796-8776 Ext. 421
21027 Crossroads Circle   262/796-1615 fax
P.O. Box 1612
Waukesha, WI 53187-1612
USA
www.artjewelrymag.com

Step by Step Beads
300 Chsterfield Parkway   610/232-5700
Suite 100
Malvern, PA 19355
USA
www.stepbystepbeads.com
sbsbeads@interweave.com

Suppliers of PMC

Argentice   0870/286-3557
34 Harlech Crescent
Sketty
Swansea
SA2 9LN
www.argentice.co.uk

FullMoons Cauldron   01344/627-945
PO Box 2173   0709/210-311
Ascot
Berkshire, SL5 0PQ
www.fullmoons-cauldron.co.uk

Silver Alchemy Marketing   0208/455-3132
Crowndean House   0208/455-5296 fax
26, Bruton Lane
Mayfair, London, W1X 7LA
www.silveralchemy.co.uk

Chununga Tree
www.chunungatree.com

The PMC Studio   0870/8500-151
17 Chiltern Business Centre
63-65 Woodside Road
Amersham
Bucks, HP6 6AA
www.pmc.vpam.co.uk
info@thepmcstudio.com

PMC Supply   07723/620-344
Ms Debra Gristwood
2 Carvear Moor
Par, PL24 2TB
www.pmc-supply.co.uk
debgristwood@dsl.pipex.com

Sutton Tools   0121/236-7139
Thomas Sutton (B'ham) Ltd.
37-38 Frederick Street
Birmingham, B1 3HN
www.suttontools.co.uk

Suppliers

Argentice   0870/286-3557
34 Harlech Crescent
Sketty
Swansea
SA2 9LN
www.argentice.co.uk

Ballou Findings   01908 569 311
15 Cochran Close
Crownhill
Milton Keynes
MK8 0AJ
www.ballou.com

Bellore Ltd.   0207/404-3220
39 Greville Street
London, EC1N 8PJ

J. Blundell & Son
16 Hatton Wall
London, EC1N 8JH

Capital Gems   0207/253-3575
30B Great Sutton Street   0207/251-9368 fax
Clerkenwell
London EC1V 0DU
www.capitalgems.com
info@capitalgems.com

Cookson Precious Metals.   0207/400-6500
43 Hatton Garden
London, EC1N 8EE
www.cooksongold.com

craftsgemz.co.uk   01422/244-389
PO Box 711
Halifax, HX2 8WU
West Yorkshire
www.craftgemz.co.uk
info@craftgemz.co.uk

Europ Findings
5-9 Hatton Wall
London, EC1N 8HX
www.eurunts.co.uk

Exchange Findings   0207/831-7574
49 Hatton Garden   0207/430-2028 fax
London, EC1N 8YS
www.cooksgold.com/trade-hatton.htm

Kernowcraft Rocks and Gems Ltd   01872/573-888
Bollingey   01872/573-704 fax
Perranporth
Cornwall, TR6 0DH
www.kernowcraft.co.uk
info@kernowcraft.com

Rainbow Silks   01494/862-111
85 High Street   01494/862-651 fax
Great Missenden
Bucks, HP16 0AL
www.rainbowsilks.co.uk
caroline@rainbowsilks.co.uk

Rashbel Marketing   0207/831-5646
24-28 Hatton Wall
London, EC1N 8JH
www.rashbel.com
order@rashbel.com

Sutton Tools   0121/236-7139
Thomas Sutton (B'ham) Ltd.
37-38 Frederick Street
Birmingham, B1 3HN
www.suttontools.co.uk

H.S. Walsh & Sons Ltd.   0207/242-3711
44 Hatton Garden
London, EC1N 8ER

Index